Delatic and Shallow Marine Sandstones: Sedimentation, Tectonics, and Petroleum Occurrences

Education Course Note Series #2

Robert J. Weimer
Colorado School of Mines

The AAPG Continuing Education Course Note Series
is an author-prepared publication of the
AAPG Department of Education.

All Series titled available from the:
AAPG Bookstore
P.O. Box 979
Tulsa, Oklahoma 74101

Published November 1976
Seventh Printing, March 1981

ISBN: 0-89181-151-6

Introduction

For more than 10 years, I have given special short courses on fossil fuel exploration for industry and government personnel at the Colorado School of Mines. Portions of these courses have been adapted as a basis for lecture series for the American Association of Petroleum Geologists in the Continuing Education Program. The material in this notebook relates only to lectures discussing stratigraphic principles and petroleum occurrences in deltaic and shallow marine sandstones. The lectures are designed to acquaint the participant with concepts and methods in stratigraphy and to acquaint him primarily with the U.S. literature relating to the subjects.

A lecture notebook of this type borrows from many scientists who have investigated a wide range of problems related to stratigraphy and to the occurrence of fossil fuels in sedimentary rocks. I acknowledge with deep gratitude my debt to those workers from whom I have synthesized ideas and material in order to pass on to more workers some of the intricacies of stratigraphic analysis and mineral exploration.

I express my gratitude to the following journals and publishers for permission to use published illustrations for this notebook: American Association of Petroleum Geologists; Springer Verlag; Prentice-Hall Inc.; Elsevier Publishing Company; Geological Society of America; Cornell University Press; Dowden, Hutchinson and Ross, Inc.; Gulf Coast Association of Geological Societies and Rocky Mountain Association of Geologists.

The authors of the illustrations are noted and the sources are given in the list of reference.

Robert J. Weimer
April, 1975

1

AAPG LECTURE SERIES: DELTAIC AND SHALLOW MARINE SANDSTONES:
SEDIMENTATION, TECTONICS AND PETROLEUM OCCURRENCES

PART I

GENETIC UNITS - PRINCIPLES - SEDIMENTARY STRUCTURES

PART II

SEDIMENTARY ENVIRONMENTS AND STRATIGRAPHIC MODELS:

PETROLEUM, COAL AND URANIUM OCCURRENCES

LECTURE 1

PROCESS-CONTROLLED GENETIC UNITS - A DIFFERENT
APPROACH TO STRATIGRAPHIC ANALYSIS

Introduction

The approach used in observing and describing sedimentary rocks strongly influences interpretations of the origin and distribution of stratigraphic units. This statement applies to collection of stratigraphic data, whether from outcrop, subsurface, or the indirect measurements of rock properties by geophysical methods.

Although the goal of the investigator is to be objective in describing stratigraphic data, an important part of his work is, by necessity, subjective in nature. For example, the lithology of sandstone and shale layers may be adequately described as to composition, texture, stratification, cementation, etc. But, if an interval 60 feet thick contains 13 sandstone layers with 12 intervening shale layers, time constraint on the investigator is likely to encourage the lumping of all units together and the preparation of one description as a stratigraphic unit of alternating layers of sandstone and shale. By this approach, the investigator has made a subjective decision in how best to describe the section. Therefore, any two investigators may describe sections differently with the results of each investigator strongly influenced by the approach used.

The Commonly Used System in Stratigraphic Analysis

The formation concept, so fundamental to geologic investigations, requires that stratigraphic sections be subdivided on the basis of mapable lithologic units. Thus, vertical stratigraphic sections are measured primarily to serve the stated requirement that the subdivisions must be "mapable", and usually mapable at a predetermined scale. At present, the most common mapping scale is determined by the scale used by published quadrangle maps. As the formations of one measured vertical section are mapped and correlated with those of another local section some distance away, formation contact lines are drawn between the two sections to depict the lateral distribution of the formation containing particular lithologies. By convention, the lines are straight or curving and drawn in a manner to

3

reflect the older and younger rock masses in a vertical sequence. This approach emphasizes the vertical distribution of rock masses and clearly prejudices concepts toward vertical accumulation of sediment, which promotes the concept of "layer cake geology".

In this formal system the facies concept is difficult to apply. Lithologies within a formation may change laterally, but the formation may retain the same name. In earlier work the formation name might be used both as a lithologic reference and a time-stratigraphic reference, an incorrect practice that should be strongly discouraged and discontinued.

The above system of stratigraphic analysis has served geologists well in preparing geologic maps, determining the structure of the earth's crust and reconstructing the past events on the earth as recorded by layered rocks. At the required scale of most project mapping, the stratigraphic interpretations are generalized at best, especially when described formations are in excess of 100 feet thick and diverse lithologies are lumped together for convention in mapping and description.

A Different Approach - Process-Controlled Genetic Units

To achieve greater accuracy in environmental interpretation, which relates to the origin and distribution of stratigraphic units, a different stratigraphic approach is required. Any new approach must consider every foot of a stratigraphic section, as to its origin, and provide for a subdivision on a natural basis, not the partially artificial and arbitrary basis, which has influenced past work.

Scientists concerned with the origin of sedimentary rocks are fortunate because they can observe the conditions and processes by which sediments accumulate today and use their observations to interpret the origin of ancient sediments. By using the areas of modern environments of deposition as natural laboratories, scientists seek to improve the quality of their work. A massive effort has been underway for the past twenty years by industry, government and university scientists to investigate modern environments of deposition and to interpret the results of the processes in Holocene sequences. Concepts have evolved from these studies that have revolutionized scientific thought about sedimentary rocks.

The results of these investigations clearly reaffirm the time-honored concept that processes within the environment of deposition control the

4

type and distribution of lithology. Therefore, newly deposited stratigraphic units can be described as process-controlled genetic units. Sediments with a common genesis have similar lithologies because the physical, biologic and chemical processes within the environment are similar.

The process-controlled genetic unit is defined as a deposit resulting primarily from the physical and biological processes operating within the environment at the time of sedimentation. The concept may be applied on a small scale (e.g. a 6 inch layer deposited by the migration of a mega ripple = a set of cross strata), or on a large scale (e.g. a 40 foot sandstone deposited by the processes associated with shoreline progradation). Normally, the concept is applied to larger scale units and, therefore, may be equivalent to facies as used by some authors. However, the selection and definition of process-controlled genetic units permit a finer subdivision and promotes keener observations than the concept of facies as generally applied. The key is to recognize lithologic differences that can be related to the stratigraphic levels at which a unique set of processes began to influence sedimentation and when they stopped (e.g. the deposits associated with the point bar of a meandering channel). The process-controlled genetic unit is almost always a smaller scale unit than a formation. The observational data, upon which the units are based, are discussed in detail in the sedimentary structure lectures. Examples of the units are illustrated in the lectures on sedimentary environments. For convenience in discussion in this notebook, the phrase "process-controlled genetic unit" is shortened to "genetic unit" which will be italicized when used in this context.

Application in Mineral Exploration

The goal of the stratigrapher is to reconstruct as accurately as possible all geologic events that are recorded by stratified rocks at any locality of interest on the earth's crust. Work to achieve this goal may be motivated on a purely philosophical basis or for economical reasons. The layered stratigraphic sequences of sedimentary rocks are vast storehouses of economic minerals. Most important are oil and gas, coal, water, uranium, but other metallic and non-metallic minerals are commonly found.

In the past the geologist has been able to predict successfully the occurrence and distribution of many types of mineral deposits based on the more general concepts and simplified methods of investigation. As the search for new mineral occurrences leads to recognition of the more subtle but equally important prospects, the investigator must develop approaches that will improve the quality and quantity of scientific work upon which predictions are made. In stratigraphic work the first step is a more accurate reconstruction of the environment of deposition of the rocks in which valuable minerals may occur. By understanding the distribution of the environment, a scientific basis is provided for prediction of extensions of known mineral occurrences, or the discovery of new ones.

If the deposit of a modern depositional environment is a <u>genetic</u> <u>unit</u>, then it follows that ancient environments, could be better interpreted by analyzing sedimentary sequences for the process-controlled genetic units. Some authors have described a similar approach by slightly different terminology. For example, Fisher and Brown, (1972), describe a genetic approach to facies analyses; and, Busch, (1971), discusses lithologic components in delta systems as "genetic increments of strata" and a larger division as a "genetic sequence of strata". Visher (1965) and Shelton (1973) use "genetic sand units" to develop conceptual models for stratigraphic studies. Whatever approach is used, it is clear that current workers in stratigraphy are making a greater effort to recognize units that have a common genesis. This approach is possible because of advances made in describing and interpreting sedimentary structures in rocks. Other lithologic features may also reflect the environment so they must be considered as well, e.g. texture, overall composition, fossil content, etc. However, if one is going to reconstruct ancient environments, the starting point is with the structures of the rock.

Much of what follows in this notebook relates to how <u>genetic</u> <u>units</u> can be recognized and used in reconstructing depositional systems to aid in mineral exploration. Emphasis will be placed on analyzing the results of studies of modern environments to determine what data and which concepts can be applied in interpreting ancient sequences. Particular attention will be given to improving both the quantitative and qualitative aspects of stratigraphic analyses.

The approach described has the greatest value in making facies analysis (predicting lateral lithologic changes in contemporaneous deposits), building stratigraphic models based on data observed in the sequence being studied, and using these techniques to predict possible mineral occurrences.

References

Busch, D. A., 1971, Genetic units in delta prospecting: Amer. Assoc.
    Petrol. Geol. Bull., v. 55, no. 8, p. 566-580.

_____, 1974, Stratigraphic traps in sandstones--exploration
    techniques: Amer. Assoc. Petrol. Geol., Memoir 21, 174 p.

Fisher, W. L. and Brown, C. F., Jr., 1972, Clastic depositional systems--a
    genetic approach to facies analysis (annotated outline and bibliography):
    Special Publication, Bureau of Econ. Geol., The Univ. of Texas at
    Austin, 211 p.

Shelton, J. W., 1973, Models of sand and sandstone deposits: Methodology
    for determining sand genesis and trend: Okla. Geol. Survey Bull. 118,
    122 p.

Visher, G. S., 1965, Use of vertical profile in environmental reconstruction:
    Amer. Assoc. Petrol. Geol. Bull., v. 49, no. 1, p. 41-61.

BOOKS RELATING TO STRATIGRAPHY AND FACIES ANALYSIS OF SANDSTONES

Amer. Assoc. Petrol. Geol. Memoir 16, Stratigraphic Oil and Gas Fields, Tulsa, Okla, 687 p.

Amer. Assoc, Petrol. Geol. Reprint Series No. 10, Facies and the Reconstruction of Environments, Tulsa, Okla.

Amer. Assoc. Petrol. Geol. Reprint Series Nos. 7 and 8, Sandstone Reservoirs and Stratigraphic Concepts, Tulsa, Okla.

*Blatt, H, Middleton, G., Murray, R., 1972, Origin of Sedimentary Rocks: Prentice-Hall, Inc., Englewood Cliffs, N. J., 643 p.

Busch, D. A., 1974, Stratigraphic Traps in Sandstones - Exploration Techniques: Amer. Assoc. Petrol. Geol. Memoir 21, 174 p.

Dunbar, C. and Rodgers, J., 1957, Principles of Stratigraphy: John Wiley and Sons, New York.

Grabau, A. W., 1960, Principles of Stratigraphy, vols. 1 and 2, Dover, New York, p. 1-581 and p. 582-1185.

Krumbein, W. C. and Sloss, L. L., 1963, Stratigraphy and Sedimentation: W. H. Freeman and Co., San Francisco, 660 p.

Pettijohn, F. J., 1957, Sedimentary Rocks: 2nd Ed., Harper and Bros., New York, 718 p.

*Pettijohn, F. J., Potter, P. E. and Siever, R., 1972, Sand and Sandstone, Springer-Verlag, New York, 618 p. (especially pages 15-23 which contain general source materials for the study of sand and sandstone including description of non-English references and textbooks).

Potter, P. E. and Pettijohn, F. J., 1963, Paleocurrents and Basin Analysis: Academic Press, Inc., New York, 296 p.

*Selley, R. C., 1971, Ancient Sedimentary Environments: Cornell Univ. Press, Ithaca, N. Y., 240 p.

Shaw, A. B., 1964, Time in Stratigraphy: McGraw-Hill Book Co., 365 p.

*Shelton, J. W., 1973, Models of Sand and Sandstone Deposits: A methodology for determining Sand Genesis and Trend: Okla. Geol. Survey Bull. 118, 122 p.

Sloss, L. L., Dapples, E. C. and Krumbein, W. C., 1960, Lithofacies Maps: An Atlas of the United States and Southern Canada: John Wiley and Sons, New York.

Twenhofel, W. H. and others, 1932, Treatise on Sedimentation: Wilkens and Wilkens, Baltimore, 926 p.

LECTURE 2

STRATIGRAPHIC PRINCIPLES (CONCEPTS)

Principle of Lateral Accumulation

The investigations of modern depositional environments, and associated Holocene deposits, have provided new insight as to how sediment layers are deposited and how thick wedges of sediment accumulate. Perhaps the most important single concept emerging from these studies is what I have called the "principle of lateral accumulation". Simply defined, the greatest volume of sedimentary rocks accumulates by the process of lateral accretion. The observations and interpretations of depositional environments in other lectures present abundant evidence to support this principle, but the following statements summarize the data:

a) Depositional surfaces (time-surfaces) upon which sediment accumulates are generally inclined.

b) Strata accumulate on the surfaces as genetically related units, largely by lateral accretion. A minor vertical component of accumulation results.

c) By lateral accretion and progradation, accumulation is usually in the direction of sediment transport. By these processes, depositional slopes may become oversteepened, and unstable masses may deform downslope by slump, creep or slide.

d) Vertical stacking of genetic units results from subsidence or compaction, or both.

e) Discontinuous lenses of porosity and permeability occur within the time-stratigraphic units.

In terms of petroleum exploration, the principle of lateral accumulation means that porous and permeable reservoir rock isolated by impermeable rock, (i.e. a trap for petroleum), may be found in any structural configuration--tops or flanks of anticlines, or in the bottom of synclines. If only the structural highs are drilled in an area, the resource potential in stratigraphic traps may be large, providing favorable source rock for petroleum accumulation has existed. In terms of other mineral exploration, the same statements apply if porosity and permeability is the important physical property in defining the host rock.

The principle of uniformitarianism, and the logic upon which it is founded, tells us that if Holocene sediments resulted primarily from lateral accumulation, then similar sequences in the ancient record must have resulted from similar processes. This does not imply that all processes operated in the same group, in the same manner, at the same rate, or in the same direction. But the dominant processes leave a record which makes possible the accurate reconstruction of the environment of deposition, the first step in stratigraphic interpretation.

If one applies the principle of lateral accumulation in stratigraphic studies, then the manner in which many of the traditional principles of stratigraphy are applied and used is incorrect.

Time-Honored Principles

Schenck (1961) published an article summarizing what he regarded to be the "Guiding Principles in Stratigraphy". The original statements, at the time a principle was first proposed, were re-examined and the original, or a modified statement, or both, was presented by Schenck.

The following summary of principles is quoted from Schenck's article with minor modifications in format, or additions, by me where required for clarity and consistency:

Superposition (Steno, 1669)

Modified statement: Law of superposition: The youngest strata are at top in an undisturbed sequence (Anthony, 1955, p. 83).

Horizontality (Steno, 1669)

Statement of principle: Dipping beds were once horizontal, (Woodford, 1935, p. 3).
Modified statement: Law of Horizontality: Sedimentary strata are laid down nearly horizontally and are essentially parallel to the surface upon which they accumulate. (Anthony, op. cit., p. 83).

Original Continuity (Steno, 1669)

Modified statement: Law of Original Continuity: The original continuity of water-laid sedimentary strata is terminated only by pinching out against the basin of deposition, at the time of their deposition. (Anthony, op. cit., p. 83).

Uniformitarianism (Hutton, 1785)

Statement of principle: Amid all the revolutions of the globe, the economy
of nature has been uniform...and her laws are the only things that have
resisted the general movement. The rivers and the rocks, the seas and
the continents have been changed in all their parts; but the laws which
direct these changes, and the rules to which they are subject, have re-
mained invariably the same. (Playfair, Illustrations of Huttonian
Theory of Earth, 1802, p. 421, quoted by Woodford, op. cit., p. 6).
Modified statement: The present is the key to the past.

Faunal Succession (Abbe Giraud-Soulavie, 1777)

Statement of principle: Fossils differ according to their geological ages;
fossils in lower formations are unlike those in higher beds. Fossil
floras and faunas succeed one another in a definite and determinable
order (Anthony, 1955, p. 89).

Strata Identified by Fossils (Smith, 1816)

Modified statement: Strata can be distinguished by their characteristic
fossils. (Woodford, 1935, op. cit., p. 5-6; Schenck, 1940, p. 1754-1755).

Rock-Stratigraphic and Time-Stratigraphic Units

Statement of principle: The discrimination between rock-stratigraphic (lith-
ogenetic) and time-stratigraphic units is essential for the classification
and nomenclature of sedimentary rocks.

Summarized statements (by Weimer):
Rock-stratigraphic Unit (Powell, 1888). The formation, as it is usually
understood today, is a local and mappable rock-stratigraphic unit--an
assemblage of rock masses grouped together for convenience in mapping
and description, generally found to constitute a genetic unit.

Time-stratigraphic unit: Rock deposited during an interval of time with time
normally defined by fossils, related to evolution, (e.g. stage or system).

Facies

Summarized statement (by Weimer): The local or particular lithologic or
biologic aspect, or both, of a time-stratigraphic unit.

The principles enunciated by Schenck are regarded as the foundation upon
which the science of stratigraphy is based. Although not discussed by Schenck,
the stratigraphic terminology, and the concepts contained therein, are for-
malized by current workers as "Codes of Stratigraphic Nomenclature". Published
by various commissions throughout the world, the Codes represent current
thought about the definition and use of principles. My opinion of present
Codes is that the principles are used in a manner which emphasizes the

vertical aspects of sediment accumulation. This is understandable because nearly all observations of stratigraphic sections are in a vertical profile (perpendicular to bedding). Sections are measured at localities of best exposure (frequently, the only exposure) and individual layers are traced laterally only in unique situations (such as cliff exposures). Therefore, the relation of one local section to another some distance away is established by correlation—the arbitrary and subjective establishment of the mutual time relationships between the sections.

Like the surface data, subsurface information is primarily point control taken from bore holes. With recent developments in continuous profiling in the reflection geophysics it is now possible, in some sequences, to make seismic observations relating the strata in one well with those of another, or to determine lateral changes in strata where no wells exist.

Recommendations

I believe that Schenck's list of principles falls into two categories: One is related primarily to the observational phase of stratigraphic work; and, the other is a theory phase. The observation, recording and theory phases of stratigraphic work may be summarized as follows:

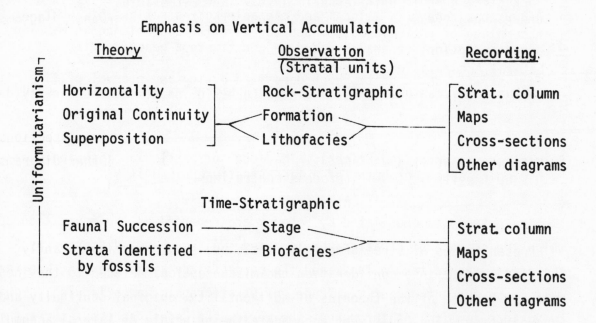

Using the theories of horizonality, original continuity and superposition, workers tend to emphasize formations as layers stacked on top of one

another. If time-stratigraphic units can be recognized (usually a difficult task), lateral changes called facies can be delineated and mapped,
either in the lithologies (lithofacies) or the paleontology (biofacies).
The American Code of Stratigraphic Nomenclature does not define the term
facies, or relate it to other rock-stratigraphic terms, despite the fact
that facies is one of the most commonly used terms by investigators describing changes in stratified rocks.

The principle of lateral accumulation is in partial or direct conflict
with the usual application of the theories of horizontality, original continuity and superposition. When applying the results of studies of modern
depositional systems to ancient sequences, the observation, recording and
theory stages must be significantly modified if lateral accumulation is
considered as the dominant process by which sediment accumulates, I propose
the following scheme:

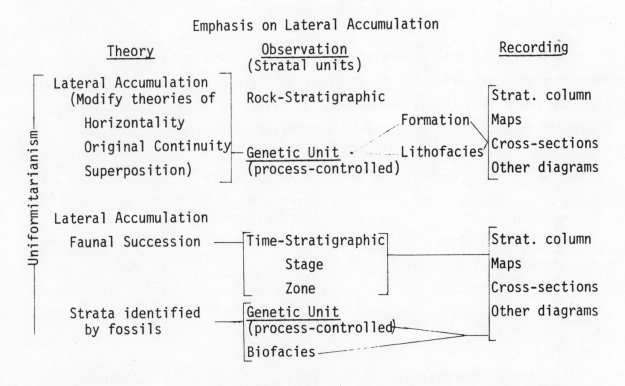

Present Codes of Stratigraphic Nomenclature should be significantly
modified to take into consideration the misconceptions related to the incorrect application of the theories of horizontality, original continuity and
superposition. The Codes must accomodate the principle of lateral accumulation and the havoc it renders to pet definitions of scientific terms and
concepts perpetuated by the commissions.

13

References

Schenck, H. G., 1961, Guiding principles in stratigraphy: Jour. Geol. Soc. India, v. 2, p. 1-10.

Codes of Stratigraphic Nomenclature

American Commission on Stratigarphic Nomenclature: Code of Stratigraphic Nomenclature: printed by the Amer. Assoc, Petrol. Geol., Box 979, Tulsa, Okla. 74101.

International Subcommission on Stratigraphic Classification Report No. 7, An International Guide to Stratigraphic Classification, Terminology and Usage: Lethaia, 1972, Universitets-forlaget, Box 307, Blindern, Oslo 3, Norway; Box 142, Boston, Mass. 02113.

CLASSIFICATION OF INTERNAL STRUCTURES

Rocks are named and classified based on composition and texture. There-fore, emphasis in training students to write lithologic descriptions is placed in recognizing and describing details of texture and composition, usually from a study of small hand specimens. In advanced courses in pet-rology the student learns to describe in even more detail the composition and texture of rocks using thin sections or disaggregated samples. Sedi-mentary structures tend to be "brushed over lightly" for two major reasons. First, they are not an integral part of any scheme for classifying rocks; and second, structures may not be an obvious feature in the small hand specimens collected for study suites. Yet sedimentary structures yield some of the most valuable data for interpreting the environment of deposition of the rock. The structures are often the only way to define the processes by which sediment is deposited. They are especially useful in determining the energy level and direction of flow of the transporting medium, biological activity (suggesting water salinities) and in delineating primary and secon-dary chemical changes in the sediment. Thus, the geologist who wishes to reconstruct environments of deposition of ancient sequences must acquire knowledge in how to recognize, describe and interpret sedimentary structures.

For convenience the internal structures in sedimentary rocks will be discussed in later lectures as inorganic, deformational and biogenic stru-ctures. All three categories may be interrelated in some layers, or only one or two may be present. Inorganic structures reflect the processes by which stratification is formed, whereas biogenic and deformational structures give insight as to processes by which stratification is modified or destroyed.

A generalized classification of sedimentary structures is presented as Table 4.1. The reader is referred to the list of books relating to sedi-mentary structures at the end of this lecture for definitions, descriptions and pictures of the structures listed.

Table 4.1.   Classification of Primary Sedimentary Structures

Inorganic Structures

Observed on bedding planes or in cross section
a) Beds or laminae (horizontal)
b) Cross-beds or cross laminae
   1) Trough
   2) Tabular or tabular planar
c) Graded beds
d) Mud cracks
e) Oxidized zones (with or without root systems)

Primarily observed on bedding planes (from Blatt, et al., 1972)
f) Tool marks
        including striations,
                  grooves,
                  brush, prod, bounce and roll marks
g) Scour marks
        including flutes
                  large scours ("cut and fill" channels)
                  rill marks, crescentic marks ("current crescents")
h) Bed forms
        including ripples, dunes, antidunes
                  grain lineation, harrow marks
                  swash marks and other wave marks

Deformational structures

a) Soft sediment folding and faulting
b) Convolute laminations
c) Ball and pillow structures
d) Diapiric structures
     mud or sand diapirs, dikes, or sills
e) Load structures
f) Gas release structures

Biogenic structures (from Frey, 1973)

	Simplified classif. based on feeding (or burrowing) habit of organism (Weimer)
a) Biogenic sedimentary structure (from Seilacher, 1953) 1) Bioturbation structures	
resting traces=cubichinia crawling traces=repichnia grazing traces=pascichnia	Grazing
feeding structures=fodinichnia	Deposit-feeding
dwelling structures=domichnia	Suspension-feeding
2) Biostratification structure	
b) Bioerosion structure	Boring
c) Root systems	

INORGANIC STRUCTURES

Soils as Sedimentary Structures and Source of Sediment

Detrital sedimentary rocks result from erosion, transportation and deposition of sediment. Although most sedimentary structures are formed during or soon after deposition of sediment, soil horizons, one of the more important structures, may develop in situ by weathering in the source area, or by periodic subaerial exposure in some environments of deposition. Typical layering of different composition and texture, making up soil profiles, may be designated as horizons A, B and C, or by greater subdivisions such as A_1, A_2, B, C, D (Fig. 5.3). The great variation of soil profiles on the earth's surface today is summarized by Fig. 5.2 reflecting the highly variable climatic and other conditions.

The soils formed by weathering in highland areas are the source for sediment caught up in transport systems. Thus, the material that forms in the soil profile, under different weathering conditions, may control the composition of the sediment in a new sedimentary cycle. In addition, porosity and permeability may be destroyed or reduced in sediment or rocks on which soil profiles develop by the leaching of material in the higher A horizon and concentration in the lower horizons B or C. Carbonate, clay, iron, silica and other cements may form by this process. For these reasons the geologist should know about modern soil processes, of the recognition of ancient soil profiles or oxidation surfaces as a type of sedimentary structure, and of the importance of paleosoils in controlling the composition, texture and color in ancient sequences.

Not all soil processes reduce porosity and permeability in reservoir rocks. The solution of carbonates may enhance porosity and permeability by producing caves, cavities, breccias, etc. Residual iron-and clay- rich soils (terra rosa) commonly cap zones of karst-solution. An example of these processes operating today in Florida is illustrated in Fig. 5.4. The importance of these processes in developing carbonate reservoir rock in the Mississippian Madison reservoir at Elk Basin, Wyoming is illustrated in Fig. 5.5 (McCaleb and Wayhan, 1969).

Nature of Stratification

Nearly all sedimentary rocks show some type of internal structure, the most common being stratification. Stratification is layering formed when sediment is deposited either flat or horizontal (sub-parallel) to bedding planes, or as inclined layers. McKee and Weir (1953) use the term stratification in a non-quantitative sense and restrict the term "beds" for layers greater than 1 centimeter thick, and "laminae" for layers less than 1 centimeter thick (Table 5.1).

The concept of a "set of strata" (Fig. 5.1), introduced by McKee and Weir (1953), may be defined as a structure showing internal consistency of layering parallel to bedding planes. A "set of cross'strata" has inclination of the internal layering to the bounding surfaces of the set (bedding planes). Two major types of cross-stratification are recognized. If the bounding surfaces are planar surfaces the cross-stratification is called tabular planar; and, if the surfaces are curving, the type is trough, (Fig. 5.9). Each set of strata or cross-strata is regarded as a small scale process-controlled genetic unit, a unit formed by deposition of sediment by certain processes acting over a time interval of short or long duration. Interpretations as to the origin of a set of strata or cross-strata rely on a knowledge of process by which sediment is transported and deposited.

Repetitive vertical sequences of stratification types and lithologies have been grouped into models with the origin interpreted as process-controlled. An example of the turbidite facies model described by Bouma (1962) is shown in Fig. 5.1a.

Origin of Stratification

Since the early work by Sorby (1859), geologists have described and interpreted sedimentary structures to aid in reconstructing depositional systems. The extensive literature and concepts on the subject were summarized in a symposium volume called "Primary Sedimentary Structures and Their Hydrodynamic Interpretation" (Middleton, ed., 1965). Several papers discuss the concept that flow-regime of the transporting medium controls the origin of stratification and other sedimentary structures. In the volume, flow regime is described as the range of flows with similar bed forms, resistance to flow and mode of sediment transport. It is a function of discharge, viscosity and bed form or roughness. Bed form is the configuration of the depositional interface (i.e. water-sediment contact). Stratification results from the falling of sediment from the suspended load onto the bed, or by movement of material in contact with the bed causing a migration of the bed form (e.g. a ripple migration).

A relationship exists among the energy of the transporting medium, bed form, stratification and direction of transport. Because of this, a general concept can be stated that cross strata dip in the direction of sediment transport. Harms and Fahnestock (1965, p. 111) illustrated these inter-relationships by a diagram which is reproduced as Fig. 5.8. The energy increases from the lower to upper flow regime and the bed form and type of stratification reflect the change. However, a relationship between grain size (texture) and stream power (energy) also influences the bed form and, therefore, the stratification type. For example, Fig. 5.6 (Simons, et al., 1965, p. 52) shows that in sand-size material, small ripples do not form on the bed containing coarse sand. The bed form is plane bed until the stream power is high enough to move the sand grains at which time dunes (megaripples) form on the bed.

Another relationship exists between grain diameter (texture) and flow velocity (energy) as illustrated by Fig. 5.7 (Allen, 1965). The transport and deposition of suspended load and bedload at different velocities are related to grain diameter. The viscosity of the transporting medium may be altered by temperature or sediment concentration which may significantly alter the curves.

The most common bed forms to produce cross-stratification are the ripple and megaripple (dune) forms. Allen prepared diagrams of the common types of cross-stratification (Fig. 5.11) resulting from migration of asymmetrical ripples, which vary in height and wave length from small to large and in configuration of crest from straight to sinuous. These and other types of common directional features were summarized by McDaniel (1968, Fig. 5.10).

Cross-stratification must be studied and described as 3-dimensional structures. In an outcrop face where only two dimensions are visible, or in slabbed cores, it is often difficult to reconstruct the shape and type of cross-strata. The problem with observing only small portions of a large set of cross-strata is illustrated by Fig. 5.12 from McCubbin and Brady (1969).

Early and repeated attempts by geologists to reconstruct the environment of deposition of a rock by the inorganic structures alone have failed. The reason seems obvious--stratification is a function of flow regime, and environments that have similar flow regimes have similar structures. Experience has demonstrated that the environment of deposition can be reconstructed accurately only when the investigator considers the vertical and lateral sequences of structures and textures, directional properties, overall lithologies, presence or absence of organic structures and other fossils.

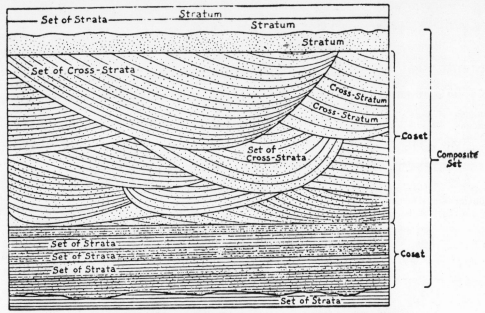

FIG. 5.1 TERMINOLOGY OF STRATIFIED AND CROSS-STRATIFIED UNITS

Table 5.1 COMPARISON OF QUANTITATIVE TERMS USED IN DESCRIBING LAYERED ROCKS

Terms to describe stratification		Terms to describe cross-stratification		Thickness	Terms to describe splitting property
Very thick-bedded		Very thickly cross-bedded		Greater than 120 cm.	Massive
Thick-bedded	Beds	Thickly cross-bedded	Cross-beds	120 cm. (about 4 ft.) to	Blocky
Thin-bedded		Thinly cross-bedded		60 cm. (about 2 ft.) to	Slabby
Very thin-bedded		Very thinly cross-bedded		5 cm. (about 2 in.) to	Flaggy
Laminated	Laminae	Cross-laminated	Cross-laminae	1 cm. (about ½ in.) to	Shaly (claystone, siltstone) Platy (sandstone, limestone)
Thinly laminated		Thinly cross-laminated		2 mm (about .08 in.) or less	Papery

After McKee and Weir, 1953

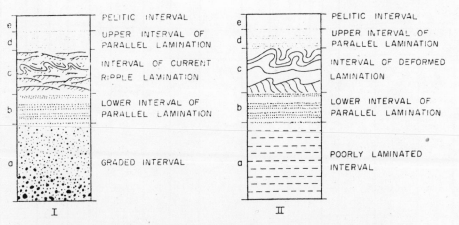

FIG. 5.1a Turbidite facies model (T_{a-e}) as originally published by Bouma (1962).

II: Turbidite facies model after Van der Lingen. Redrawn after Van der Lingen (1969).

21

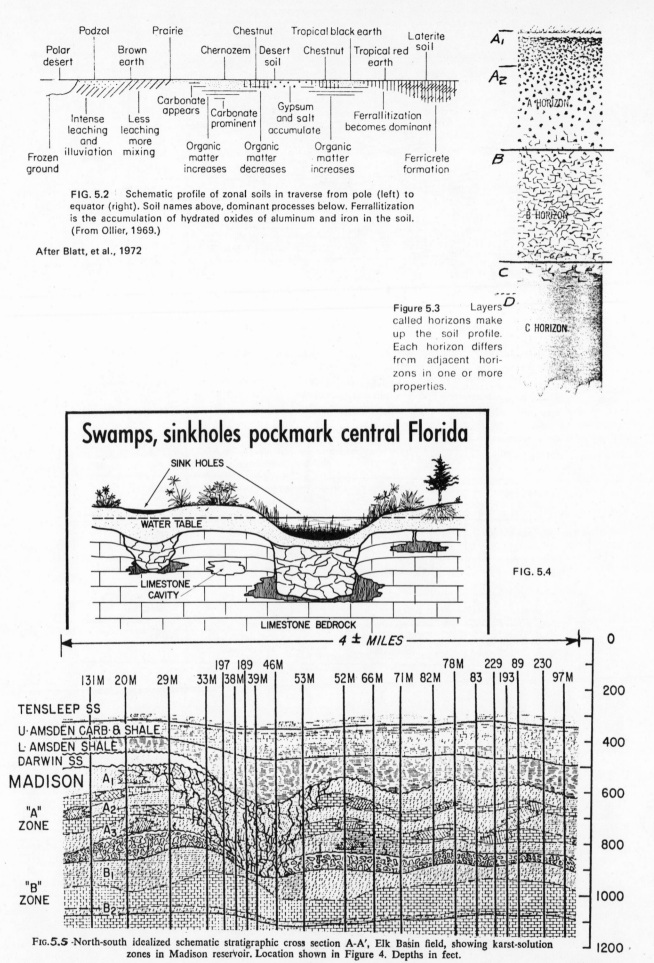

FIG. 5.2 Schematic profile of zonal soils in traverse from pole (left) to equator (right). Soil names above, dominant processes below. Ferrallitization is the accumulation of hydrated oxides of aluminum and iron in the soil. (From Ollier, 1969.)

After Blatt, et al., 1972

Figure 5.3 Layers called horizons make up the soil profile. Each horizon differs from adjacent horizons in one or more properties.

Swamps, sinkholes pockmark central Florida

FIG. 5.4

FIG. 5.5 North-south idealized schematic stratigraphic cross section A-A', Elk Basin field, showing karst-solution zones in Madison reservoir. Location shown in Figure 4. Depths in feet.

22

After McCaleb & Wayhan, 1969

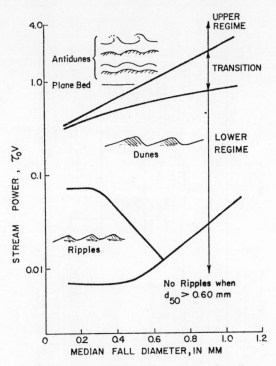

FIG. 5.6 Relation of stream power and median
fall diameter to form of bed roughness.

After Simons, et al., 1965

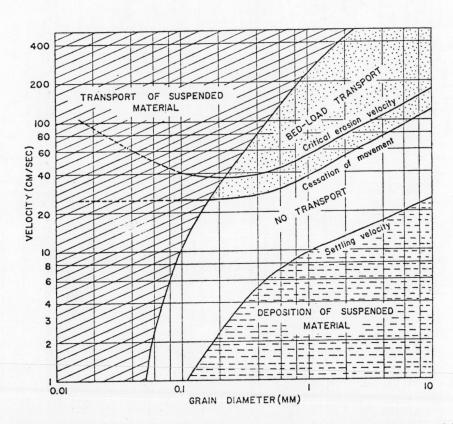

FIG. 5.7 Relation between flow velocity, grain size, and state of sediment in uniform material of 2.65
g/cm³, for flow velocity 1 m above bottom. (Modified after SUNDBORG, 1956, fig.23.)

From Allen, 1965

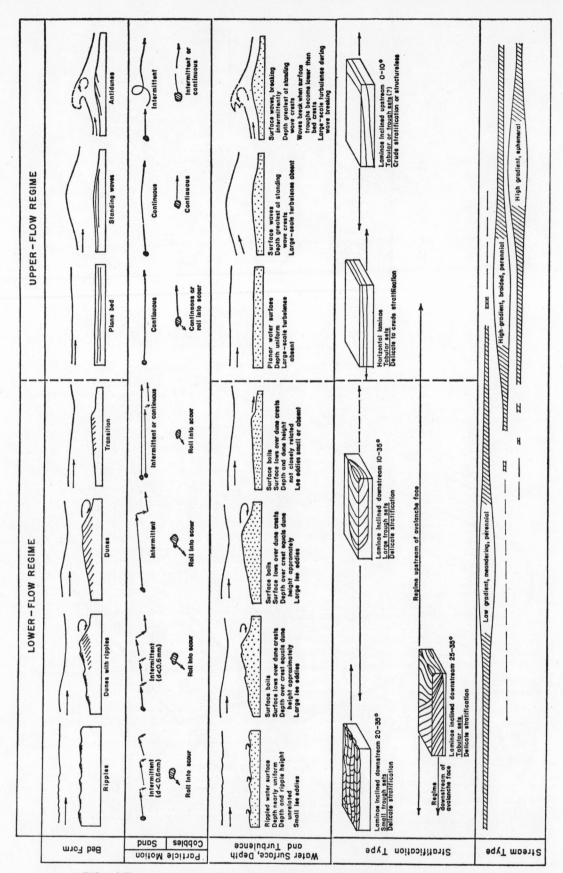

FIG. 5.8 Flow regime diagram for sand beds (Harms, J. C. and R. K. Fahnestock, 1965).

24

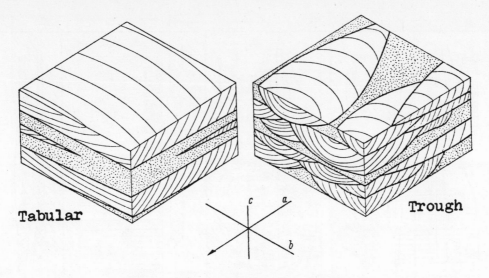

FIG. 5.9—The two main types of cross stratification

SEDIMENTARY DIRECTIONAL FEATURES

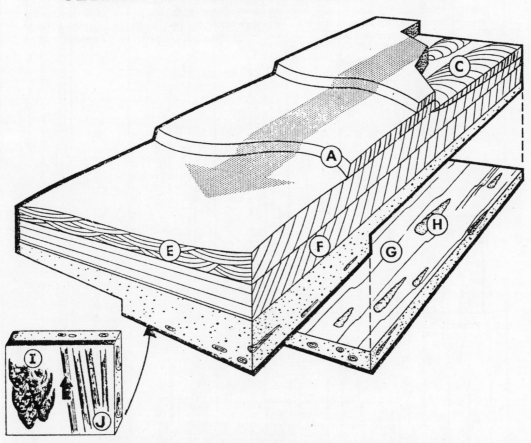

FIG. 5.10 Sedimentary directional features. Letters refer to Table I. *A*, Asymmetrical ripple mark; *C*, rib and furrow; *E*, festoon cross-bedding; *F*, planar cross-bedding; *G*, parting lineation; *H*, fossil lineation; *I*, flute casts; *J*, striations and groove casts.

After McDaniel, 1968

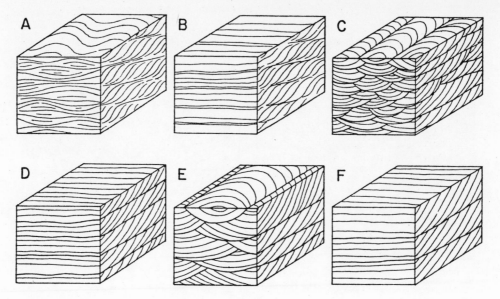

FIG. 5.11 Common types of cross-stratification considered to be generated by migration of asymmetrical ripple marks. (Based on ALLEN, 1963a, b.) A. Small scale cross-stratified sets showing "pinch and swell" structure and gradational contacts resulting from small scale linguoid ripples. B. Cross-strata in small scale "planar" sets with gradational contacts resulting from small scale straight ripples. C. Small scale "trough" cross-stratified sets resulting from small scale linguoid ripples. D. Small scale "planar" cross-stratified sets resulting from migration of small scale straight ripples. E. Large scale "trough" cross-stratified sets resulting from large scale lunate and possibly linguoid ripples. F. Large scale "planar" cross-stratified sets resulting from straight large scale ripples.   From Allen, 1965

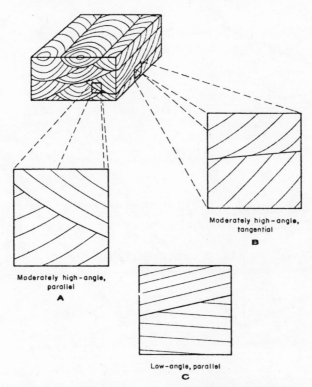

Moderately high-angle,
tangential
B

Moderately high-angle,
parallel
A

Low-angle, parallel
C

FIG. 5.12 Major types of cross-stratification in UA-5 sandstone. A and B are believed to represent the same type of cross-stratification, as it appears on surfaces cut perpendicular to the trough axes (A) and parallel to the trough axes (B); a reconstruction of the three-dimensional form of the sets is shown by the block diagram. The type shown by C appears low angle and parallel on surfaces cut in various orientations; the three-dimensional form of the sets is not known.

From McCubbin and Brady 1969

PUBLICATIONS RELATING TO INORGANIC STRUCTURES

Allen, J. R. L., 1965, A review on the origin and characteristics of recent alluvial sediments, Sedimentology, v. 5, p. 89-191.

Blatt, H., Middleton, G. and Murray, R., 1972, Origin of sedimentary rocks, Prentice-Hall, Inc., Englewood Cliffs, N. J.

*Frey, R. W., 1973, Concepts in the study of biogenic sedimentary structures, Jour. Sed. Petrology, v. 43, no. 1, p. 1-19.

Harms, J. C. and Fahnestock, R. K., 1965, Stratification, bed forms, and flow phenomena (with an example from the Rio Grande, Soc. Econ. Paleo. and Min., Sp. Pub. 12, p. 84-115.

McCaleb, J. A. and Wayhan, D. A., 1969, Geologic reservoir analysis, Mississippian Madison Formation, Elk Basin Field, Wyoming-Montana, Amer. Assoc. Petrol. Geol. Bull., v. 53, no. 10, p. 2094-2113.

McCubbin, D. G. and Brady, M. J., 1969, Depositional environments of the Almond reservoirs, Patrick Draw Field, Wyoming, The Mountain Geologist, v. 6, no. 1, p. 3-26.

McDaniel, G. A., 1968, Application of sedimentary features and scalar properties to hydrocarbon exploration, Amer. Assoc. Petrol. Geol., Bull. v. 52, p. 1689-1699.

*McKee, E. P. and Weir, G. W., 1953, Terminology for stratification and cross-stratification in sedimentary rocks, Geol. Soc. Bull., v. 64, p. 381-389.

Meckel, L. D., 1967, Tabular and trough cross-bedding: comparison of deep azimuth variability, Jour. Sed. Pet., v. 37, p. 80-86.

*Middleton, G. V. (ed.), 1965. Primary sedimentary structures and their hydrodynamic interpretation, Soc. Econ. Paleo., Sp. Pub. 12, 265 p.

Sielacher, A., 1964, Biogenic sedimentary structures in Imbrie, J. and Newell, N. D. (eds.), Approaches to Paleoecology, John Wiley and Sons, New York, p. 296-316.

*Simons, D. B., Richardson, E. V. and Norden, C. F., Jr., 1965, Sedimentary structures generated by flow in alluvial channels, Soc. Econ. Paleo. and Min., Sp. Pub. 12, p. 52.

Sorby, H. C., 1859, On the structures produced by the currents present during the deposition of stratified rocks, Geol. Soc. London Quart. Jour., v. 64, p. 171-233.

LECTURE 5

DEFORMATIONAL STRUCTURES

Processes

Sediment layers may be deformed after deposition and before lithification while still in a soft-sediment state. A layer may be deposited, deformed and covered by a younger undeformed layer giving interstratal deformational structures sometimes referred to as penecontemporaneous structures. Or layers may be buried to some depth before being deformed by faulting, folding or diapiric shale movement. The most commonly observed deformational structures are tabulated in Table 4.1. The scale of disruption may vary from centimeters to kilometers in both horizontal and vertical dimensions. The intensity of the deformation may range from slight to extreme.

Processes causing deformation vary from simple to complex (Fig. 6.1). The most common force causing deformation is gravity acting upon a mass of sediment on an unstable slope causing folding and faulting by sliding, slumping and crumpling. Another common process is the loading of a low density layer (clay and water) with a higher density mass (sand and water) causing the low density material to move laterally and/or vertically producing the common load structures. The development of small scale deformational structures by loading was reported from laboratory experiments by McKee and Goldberg (1969).

Thick clay layers may be deposited that do not compact normally upon burial, i.e. they retain pore water. When loaded by younger sediments the undercompacted low density shale mass may flow, aided by abnormally high pore pressure. Mud lumps (shale diapirs), sandstone dikes, complex folds and faults, and other types of deformation in sand are related to these phenomena (Fig. 6.2). Following earlier work by Hubbert and Rubey (1959) Gretener (1969) discusses the role of high fluid pressure in deformation of sediments and describes the relationship of pore-fluid pressure to overburden pressure (Fig. 6.3). One style of growth faulting may be genetically related to large undercompacted overpressured shale masses (Bruce, 1972, see Fig. 16.22).

Gas trapped in sediment layers may develop high pressure and escape causing minor deformation, or small or large scale volcano-like structures.

The dynamics of submarine gravity transport mechanism was summarized by Dott (1963). He listed four subaqueous processes as rockfall, slides and slumps, mass flow and turbidity flow. Figure 6.1 is a summary of these processes modified by Cook, et al. (1972) and adapted to carbonate rocks.

Deformation in Delta Front - Prodelta Environment

A region with high rates of sedimentation compared to marginal areas is referred to as a depocenter (Fig. 6.6). One of the modern environments associated with a depocenter in which pene-contemporaneous deformation is commonly observed is in the delta front-prodelta environment. High rates of sedimentation in the shallow water region cause progradation and oversteepening of the depositional slope.

Coleman, et al. (1974) compiled the results of years of investigations to describe various types of deformation associated with sediments of the modern Mississippi River delta. Figures 6.6 through 6.12 from these authors illustrate the modern Mississippi River Delta and describe some of the deformational processes. In the following abstract, Coleman and Wright (1974) summarize deformational processes in delta front deposits:

River-mouth depositional patterns are modified by sediment deformational processes of sufficient magnitude to endanger severely bottom-supported structures. Several types of deformations are present and include (a) peripheral slumping, (b) differential weighting and diapirism, (c) graben faulting, (d) mass wasting by sediment degassing, and (e) deep-seated flowage. High depositional rates are present near the river mouth and decrease seaward; with time, the bar front oversteepens and rotational slump planes form peripheral to the bar front, moving sediment into deeper water. These blocks have longitudinal dimensions of approximately 200 to 2,000 ft. and lateral dimensions of 600 to greater than 2,000 ft. Differential loading by denser bar sands overlying low-density clays results in vertical and seaward flowage of the clays contemporaneously with seaward bar progradation. Diapiric folds and spines (mudlumps)

30

intrude into delta-front sediments on the seaward side of the
deforming load, vertical movement affecting sediments to depths
in excess of 500 ft. The seaward extrusion and continued movement
of clays arch the overlying delta-front sediments, and this stress
is relieved by small graben faults oriented radially to the deforming load or delta lobe. The grabens have widths from 150 to 1,500
ft. and lengths of several miles. The finer grained river-mouth
sediments contain high percentages of methane and CO_2 gases, formed
by bacterial decomposition of organics. Passage of hurricane waves
produces bottom-pressure perturbations, forcing the entrapped gas
upward causing loss of sediment strength and allowing mass movement.
The weight of the modern delta has depressed underlying Pleistocene
sands about 400 ft. causing squeezing and flowage of clays onto the
continental shelf at water depths greater than 300 ft. Large-scale
slumping and faulting near the continental shelf result from this
clay flowage. These processes are contemporaneous with deposition
and play an important role in initiating a depocenter.

Many papers in literature describe the association of delta front sedimentation and deformation in modern deltas. Most notable are by Mathews and
Shepard (1962) on the Fraser River Delta, B. C.; Shepard (1973), and Shepard,
Dill and Heezen (1968) on the Magdelena Delta, Colombia; and Burke (1972) on
the Niger. Bea (1971) described the results of one slump movement on the
front of the Mississippi Delta at South Pass Block 70, 10 miles east of South
Pass. Two rigs on drilling location were displaced and the holes lost when
a sea floor slump block in 300 feet of water moved downslope and seaward during Hurricane Camille.

Delta front deformation in ancient sequences has been described in the
Cretaceous of the Rocky Mountains area by Howard and Lohrengell (1969),
Hubert, et al. (1972) and Weimer (1973); the Eocene of Oregon by Dott (1966);
the Cretaceous of Brazil by Klein et al. (1972); and the Pennsylvanian of
Texas by Galloway and Brown, (1972).

Deformation in Other Environments

An interesting example of mud deformation by loading is reported by
Brown (1968) in the Coorong Lagoon, South Australia. Sand dunes entering the
lagoon from the shoreline are producing deformational structures as they
traverse lagoonal muds. At the base of the encroaching dune, the muds are
forced into a series of sub-parallel anticlinal ridges 1 m to 3 m wide and
.5 m high. Distance between adjacent ridges varies from 1 m to 7 m. One area
affected is 150 m wide and 1500 m long.

Similar deformation associated with ancient dune fields has been observed

31

by me in the Carmel Formation in the Arches National Monument, Utah. Shales and sandstones of the Carmel are deformed over a large area where they underlie the Entrada sandstone of eolian origin. Differential loading by large migrating sand dunes apparently caused the deformation.

Deformational structures of many types and scales are found in ancient deep water marine sediments. The vertical repetitive sequence of structures in turbidites, described as the Bouma sequence (Fig. 5.1a) contains small scale deformed layers in the C zone above the graded bed (A) and the zone of parallel laminations (B). Large scale slumps producing complex folding and faulting similar to delta front slumps also occur in turbidites or in other type deposits of submarine fans. Many slumps are probably due to oversteepening of the depositional surface by higher rates of sedimentation in the proximal area than in the distal area resulting in unstable masses moving downslope.

Convoluted bedding has been observed in many environments, but a common occurrence is in point bar and other types of fluvial sandstones. The tops of sets of cross strata are overturned and deformed in the direction of sediment transport. Although not clearly understood, the structures may form during the change in flow regime from a flood peak to non-flood stage of flow in the channel.

Slumps and slides involving both shale and sand layers are reported by Meckel and others in the partial abandonment-fill of straight distributary channels. The deformation may occur as bank collapse into the channel, as slumps of the active fill (sand bars) and overlying clay and silt layers, or as the breakup of clay layers by an unknown process within the channel. The change in the lithology of a distributary fill from an active to abandoned phase, and the associated deformation, will be discussed in Lecture 11 on deltas (Fig. 11.25).

A study of deformational structures in modern environments clearly indicates that the penecontemporaneous deformation of sediments is a common and widespread phenomenon. These observations lead me to believe that this type of deformation is far more common in ancient sequences than generally recognized by geologists. The type and style of deformation give important clues as to processes operating within environments of deposition, especially as to varying rates of sedimentation.

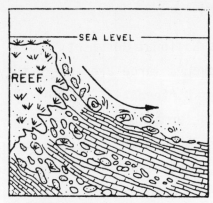

SUBMARINE ROCKFALL

- Rolling or freefall of individual clasts.
- Sand to boulder-sized clasts.
- Depositional units usually show distinct boundaries.
- Poor sorting, no grading.
- Interclast porosity.
- Transport distance short across steep angles.

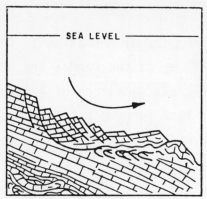

SUBMARINE SLIDE & SLUMPS

- Displacement of coherent masses.
- Movement along discrete shear planes.
- Little or no internal flow.
- Local folds and faults

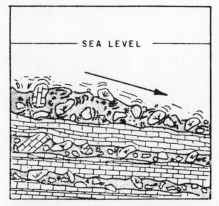

SUBMARINE MASS FLOW

- Depositional units show distinct boundaries.
- Planar base and top, or planar base and hummocky top.
- Poor sorting; normal grading rare.
- Usually has a mud matrix.
- Clasts jumbled together during movement and supported by some type of non-turbulent mechanism.
- Transport distance intermediate across low angle slopes.

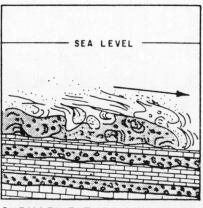

SUBMARINE TURBIDITY FLOW

- Depositional units usually show distinct boundaries.
- Planar base and top, or channeled base and planar top.
- Variable sorting; normal grading and other Bouma sequences common
- May or may not have a mud matrix
- Clasts jumbled together during movement and supported by turbulent suspension.
- Transport distance far across low angle slopes.

FIG. 6.1   Major types of submarine gravity transport mechanisms and some descriptive and interpretive characteristics (modified after R. H. Dott, Jr., 1963).

Cook, et al., 1972

33

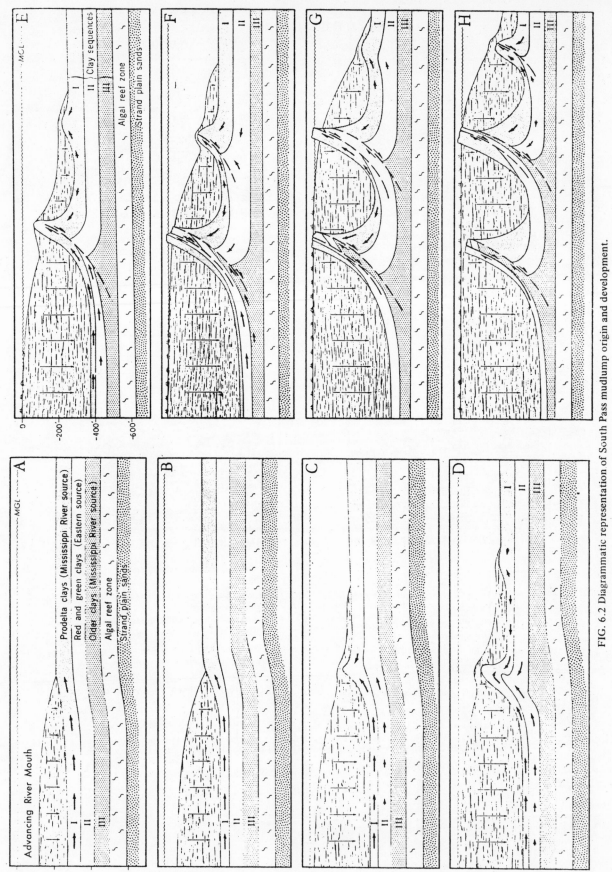

FIG. 6.2 Diagrammatic representation of South Pass mudlump origin and development.

From Morgan, et al., 1968

Key (panel A):

Advancing River Mouth

I Prodelta clays (Mississippi River source)
II Red and green clays (Eastern source)
III Older clays (Mississippi River source)
   Algal reef zone
   Strand plain sands

Key (panel E):

MGL

I Prodelta clays (Mississippi River source)
II Clay sequences
III
   Algal reef zone
   Strand plain sands

34

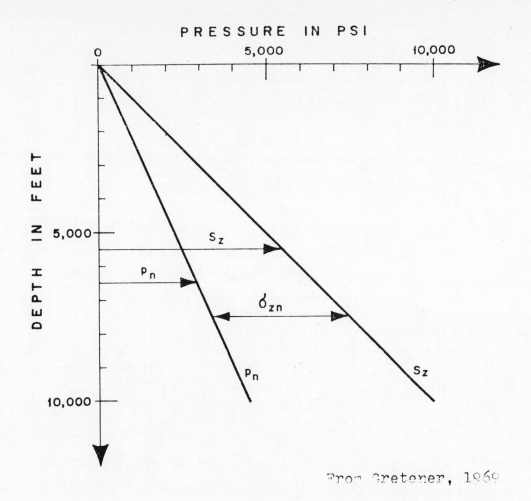

From Gretener, 1969

FIG. 6.3 Total overburden pressure (S_z), pore-fluid pressure (p_n) and effective overburden pressure (σ_{zn}) versus depth for normal conditions under the assumption that $\rho_b = 2.3$ g/cm³ and $\rho_w = 1.04$ g/cm³.

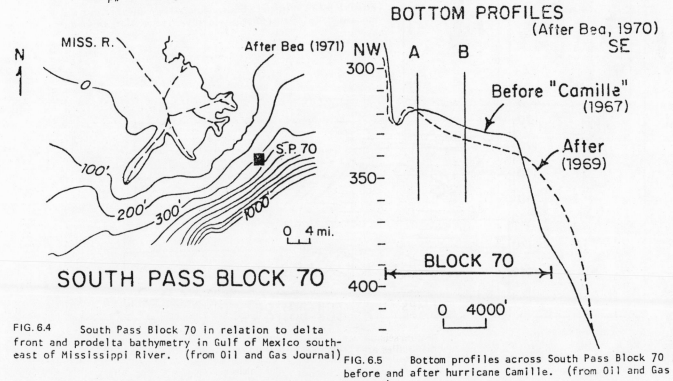

FIG. 6.4   South Pass Block 70 in relation to delta front and prodelta bathymetry in Gulf of Mexico southeast of Mississippi River.   (from Oil and Gas Journal)

FIG. 6.5   Bottom profiles across South Pass Block 70 before and after hurricane Camille.   (from Oil and Gas Journal)

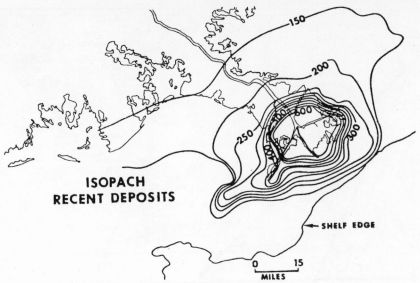

ISOPACH
RECENT DEPOSITS

← SHELF EDGE

0   15
MILES

FIG. 6.6   Isopach map of the Recent sediments (sediments younger than 30,000 years in the Mississippi River delta).

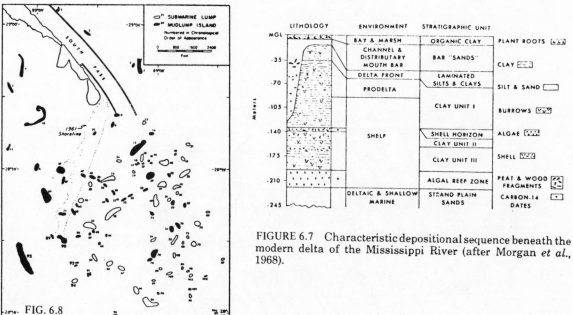

FIGURE 6.7   Characteristic depositional sequence beneath the modern delta of the Mississippi River (after Morgan *et al.*, 1968).

FIG. 6.8

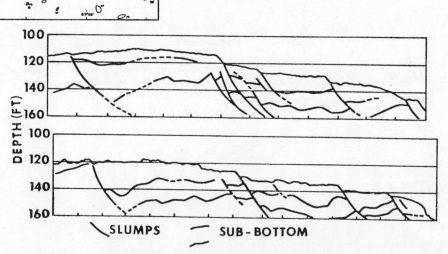

FIGURE 6.9   Tracing from seismic profiles showing peripheral faults and slumps that scar the delta platform. Profiles are spaced 600 meters apart.

After Coleman, et al., 1974

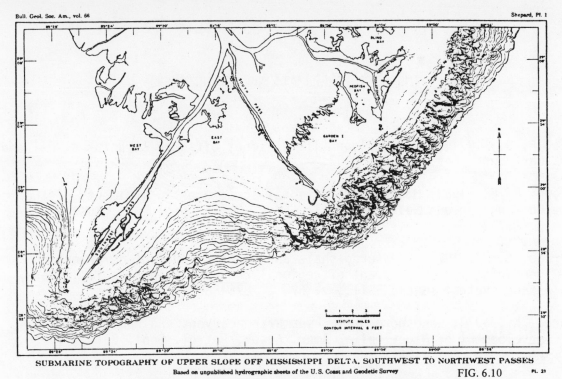

SUBMARINE TOPOGRAPHY OF UPPER SLOPE OFF MISSISSIPPI DELTA, SOUTHWEST TO NORTHWEST PASSES
Based on unpublished hydrographic sheets of the U.S. Coast and Geodetic Survey   FIG. 6.10   PL. 21

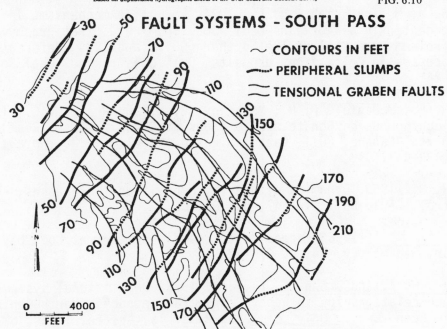

FAULT SYSTEMS - SOUTH PASS

~ CONTOURS IN FEET
 PERIPHERAL SLUMPS
 TENSIONAL GRABEN FAULTS

FIGURE 6.11   Map showing special relationship of deformational patterns on the delta platform. The region is located just southeast of the mouth of South Pass.

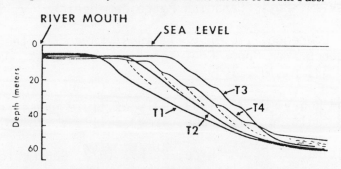

FIGURE 6.12 Diagrammatic representation of development of peripheral slumps on the delta platform.

After Coleman, et al., 1974

37

Bea, R. G., 1971, How sea floor slides affect offshore structures, Oil and Gas Jour., Nov. 29, p. 88-92.

Brown, R. G., 1969, Modern deformational structures in sediments of the Coorong Lagoon, South Australia, Spec. Publs. Geol. Soc. Aust., 2, p. 237-241.

* Bruce, C. M., 1973, Pressured shale and related sediment deformation: mechanism for development of regional contemporaneous faults, Amer. Assoc. Petrol. Geol. Bull., v. 57, p. 876-886.

Burke, K., 1972, Longshore drift, submarine canyons and submarine fans in development of Niger Delta, Amer. Assoc. Petrol. Geol. Bull., v. 56, no. 10, p. 1975-1984.

*Coleman, J. M. and Wright, L. D., 1974, Formative mechanisms in a modern depocenter in New Orleans Geol. Soc. Sp. Pub., Stratigraphy and Petroleum Potential of the Northern Gulf, and 1974, Deformational processes in delta front deposits, Gulf Coast Assoc. Geol Soc. Trans., v. 24.

Cook, H. E., McDaniel, P. N., Mountjoy, E. W. and Pray, L. C., 1972, Allochthonous carbonate debris flows at Devonian Bank (Reef) Margins, Alberta, Canada, Bull. Canadian Petrol. Geol., v. 20, no. 3, p. 439-497.

*Dott, R. H., 1963, Dynamics of gravity depositional processes, Amer. Assoc. Petrol. Geol. Bull., v. 47, p. 104-108.

_____, 1966, Eocene deltaic sedimentation at Coos Bay, Oregon, Jour. Geology, v. 74, p. 373-420.

Galloway, W. E. and Brown, L. F., Jr., 1972, Depositional systems and shelf-slope relationships in upper Pennsylvanian rocks, North Central Texas, Bur. Econ. Geol., Univ. of Texas R. I. 75, Austin, Texas, 62 p.

*Gretener, P. E., 1969, Fluid pressure in porous media--its importance in geology--a review, Bull. Canadian Petroleum Geology, v. 17, p. 283-289.

Howard, J. D. and Lohrengell, C. F., II, 1969, Large non-tectonic deformational structures from Upper Cretaceous rocks of Utah, Jour. Sed. Petrology, v. 39, p. 1032-1039.

Hubbert, M. K. and Rubey, W. W., 1959, Role of fluid pressure in mechanics of overthrust faulting, Geol. Soc. Amer. Bull., v. 70, p. 115-166.

Hubert, J. F., Butera, J. G. and Rice, R. F., 1972, Sedimentology of Upper Cretaceous Cody-Parkman delta, southwestern Wyoming, Geol. Soc. Amer. Bull., v. 83, p. 1649-1670.

Klein, G. D., de Melo, Ubirajara, and Farera, J. C., 1972, Subaqueous gravity processes on the front of Cretaceous deltas, Reconcavo Basin, Brazil, Geol. Soc. Amer. Bull., v. 83, p. 1469-1492.

McKee, E. D., and Goldberg, M., 1969, Experiments on formation of contorted structures in mud, Geol. Soc. Amer. Bull., v. 80, p. 231-244.

*Morgan, J. P., Coleman, J. M and Gagliano, S. M., 1968, Mud-lumps: diapiric structures in Mississippi Delta sediments, Amer. Assoc. Petrol. Geol., Memoir No. 8, p. 145-161.

Shepard, F. P., 1955, Delta front valleys bordering Mississippi distributaries, Geol. Soc. Amer. Bull., p. 1489-1498.

_____, 1973, Sea floor off Magdalena delta and Santa Marta area, Colombia, Geol. Soc. Amer. Bull., v. 84, p. 1955-1972.

Shepard, F. P. and Mathews, W. H. 1962, Sedimentation of Frazer Delta, British Columbia, Amer. Assoc. Petrol. Geol. Bull., v. 46, p. 1416-1443.

Shepard, F. P., Dill, R. F. and Heezen, B. C., 1968, Diapiric intrusions in foreset sediments off Magdelena Delta, Colombia, Amer. Assoc. Petrol. Geol. Bull., v. 52, p. 2197-2207.

Sorauf, J. E., 1965, Flow rolls of Upper Devonian rocks of south-central New York State, Jour. Sed. Petrology, v. 35, p. 533-563.

Sullwold, H. H., Jr., 1959, Nomenclature of load deformation in turbidites, Geol. Soc. Amer. Bull., v. 70, p. 1247-1248.

_____, 1960, Load cast terminology and origin of convolute bedding: Further comments, Geol. Soc Amer. Bull., v. 71, p. 635-636.

Tiffin, D. L., Murray, J. W., Mayers, I. R., and Garrison, R. E., 1971, Structure and origin of foreslope hills, Frazer Delta, British Columbia, Bull. Canadian Petrol. Geol., v. 19, no. 3, p. 509-600.

Ten Haaf, E., 1956, Signigicance of convolute lamination, Geol. en Mijnbouw, n. ser., v. 18, p. 188-194.

Walker, R. G., 1970, Review of the geometry and facies organization of turbidites and turbidite-bearing basins in Lajoie, J. (ed.) Flysch Sedimentation in North America, Geol. Assoc. Canada, Sp. Paper 7, 272 p.

Weimer, R. J., 1973, A guide to uppermost stratigraphy, central Front Range, Colorado: deltaic sedimentation, growth faulting and early Laramide crustal movement, The Mountain Geologist, v. 10, no. 3, p. 63-97.

BIOGENIC STRUCTURES

Introduction

Ichnology, the study of fossil and recent traces of organisms, has
expanded at an explosive rate during the past 20 years. Encouraged by
early reported successes in identifying facies by their trace fossil assemblages, workers have been re-examining reported unfossiliferous
sequences and are using biogenic sedimentary structures, together with
inorganic sedimentary structures, to expand and improve interpretations
about environments of deposition. The ichnological information may also
be useful in other studies relating to paleontology, stratigraphy and
sedimentology (Frey, 1973, Table 7.2).

Seilacher (1964) characterized trace fossils as follows: 1) long
time range; 2) narrow facies range; 3) no secondary replacement; and,
4) occurrence in otherwise non-fossiliferous rocks. Because of the new-
ness of the subject of ichnology to many geologists, several tables from
the summary article by Frey (1973) are reproduced (Tables 7.2 - 7.5).
Included are descriptions of basic concepts, definition of common terms,
major relationships among biogenic structures and a commonly used classification modified from Seilacher (1953).

An equally important article was published by Frey (1971) describing
and citing examples of the use of ichnology. Following and expanding the
early thoughts by Hantzschel (1962), Schafer (1962), Seilacher (1964, 1967),
Goldring (1964), Osgood (1970) and Crimes and Harper, eds. (1970), Frey
discussed the geologic significance of trace fossils. The reader may use
the lists of references in these articles as a guide to the trace fossil
literature.

In reconstructing depositional environments and paleoecology Frey
(1971) believes trace fossils may give clues to the following: bathymetry,
temperature and salinity, rates of deposition, amounts of sediments deposited or eroded, aeration of water and sediments, substrate coherence
and stability and sediment re-working. The reader is referred to Frey's
article for detailed discussion of these points. Of particular interest
is the use of the data to reconstruct both organic and inorganic processes

functioning within the environment during deposition of sediment.

Much work has been done on the traces in sediment produced by living organisms. Examples of a few of these are shown on Fig 7.1. The modern processes serve as the most important reference in interpreting the ancient records. The literature and some of the results are described by Frey (1971).

Recognition and Classification

The non-specialist working with trace fossils experiences several difficulties. First is the recognition and naming of the fossil; second, is the description of the structure; and third, is determining the usefulness of the fossil in interpretation.

To simplify the problem for people working with slabbed cores one approach worthy of consideration is the classification by Moore and Scruton (1957) describing layers as regular, irregular, mottles (distinct and indistinct) and homogeneous (Fig. 7.3). They interpret these original sedimentary structures as parts of a continuum caused by the progressive alteration of sediments by burrowing organisms (Fig. 7.4). The use of this simple classification is illustrated by the authors in a map showing areal distribution of minor internal structures north and east of the modern Mississippi delta (Fig. 7.5). Variation in distribution of minor structures are related to rates of deposition and other processes (Figs. 7.6 and 7.7). Near the east side of the delta regular layers occur where rates of sedimentation are high and burrowing intensity by organisms is low. Mottles, irregular layers and homogeneous structures occur on the shelf where rates of sedimentation are slow and oceanic processes predominate. A similar burrow distribution was reported in ancient rocks by Weimer (1973), Weimer and Land (1975, in press) from studies of deltaic and interdeltaic areas of sedimentation in the Cretaceous of the Western Interior of the U.S.

Another simplified approach to classifying trace fossils is by reconstructing the feeding (or burrowing) habit of the animal that left the trace. This system is most useful in working vertical sections in slabbed cores or outcrops. Depending on the shape or form of the trace, the structure may be classified in the following manner.

Table 1. Simplified classification of bioturbation and other structures

Feeding (or burrowing) habit	Type of burrow or trace
Suspension feeding	Walled-burrow structure in better sorted sand. Feeding and/or dwelling structure.
Deposit feeding	Burrows cutting or disrupting stratification in muddy sand or sandy mud; burrow may be sand or mud filled and have any orientation. Varies from slight to intense bioturbation of deposit.
Grazing	Tracks and trails mainly as bedding plane features. Includes resting and crawling traces. Sand or mud substrate.
Boring	Burrows that appear to have been cut into lithified (hard) substrate. Sand or mud filled.

The basis for this classification rests on the premise that most of the animal's activity is related to gathering a food supply, which is plant or animal-derived organic material in the sediment. With water as the transport medium, the organic material, being of low density, will tend to follow the mud in the transport and deposition processes. Thus, where currents are strong and mud and organics are in the suspension, animals will construct burrows in sand substrate. Because the sand may have bottom traction movement, or because the sand may be uncompacted, the animal constructs a wall to the burrow to maintain an open dwelling structure and prevent collapsing. The animal feeds by circulating water through the burrow network and removing organic material and clay. The clay is pelleted and used to line the burrow, or the pellets are cast back to the surface. An example of this type of feeding habit was reported for the modern decapod Callianassa major Say by Weimer and Hoyt (1964). They reported this type of process for burrow construction as responsible for the widespread fossil burrow Ophimorpha nodosa Lundgren found in marine Cretaceous and Tertiary rocks on a world-wide occurrence.

When organic material and mud settle from suspension and form a deposit, the layer contains a food supply. Organisms will burrow through the deposit to collect food, thus the reference as deposit-feeding organisms. Depending on the abundance of animals, rates of sedimentation, amount of organic matter and oxygen, the bioturbation may vary from slight, with minor disruption of stratification, to intense with complete destruction of stratification forming a homogeneous structure.

A third feeding habit of organisms is the process of the animal moving about the depositional interface and collecting food by grazing. Tracks and trails are evidence of this activity. Because of the difficulty of the non-specialist in separating resting and crawling traces from grazing traces, they are all included in this classification as grazing traces.

In many ancient sequences, bioturbation by plant burrows (i.e. root systems) is difficult to separate from bioturbation by animal activity. This is especially the case for coastal plain sedimentation where fresh and brackish-water environments are intimately related. Removal of the organics from the root systems by slight oxidation is common and the root burrows may be filled with sand. Because the root systems are generally associated with fresh water and subaerial exposure, they are important guide posts and marker horizons in environmental reconstruction. The common criteria used in recognizing root burrows are a downward tapering form, branching downward, associated burrows of many different sizes, compacted or crushed burrows, and occurrences of coalified (woody) material in burrow. Root systems are commonly associated with mud cracks or oxidized zones indicating subaerial exposure.

Use of Trace Fossils in Environmental Reconstruction

The writer's experience suggests that trace fossil distribution in ancient sequences is most useful in determining water depths and associated energy levels (bathymetry), salinity, rates of deposition, and sediment reworking (bioturbation).

The use of biogenic structures in reconstructing water depths and associated facies was described by Howard (1966, 1972) for marine Cretaceous strata in the Book Cliffs of Utah. Summary diagrams indicating the trace fossil assemblages from shallow to deeper water are shown on Figures 7.8 - 7.11. Typical trace fossils are recognized in the beach fore-shore, shoreface and offshore (Fig. 7.12). In addition, general facies are indicated that are related to changes in energy (water depth) in the

depositional environment. Similar vertical and lateral associations are reported by Land (1972) for Cretaceous marine rocks in the Rock Springs uplift, Wyoming.

Seilacher (1963) and others have proposed the concept of characteristic trace fossil assemblages reflecting paleobathymetric conditions. The
assemblages were named after common traces and the three names used for
marine water depths are: Cruziana assemblage = shallow neritic, Zoophycos
assemblage = deeper neritic to bathyal; and, Nereites assemblage = bathyal
to abyssal. These terms have been accepted by many workers, but some ob-
servers have noted that clear-cut depth boundaries between assemblages may
not exist. For example, Kern and Warme (1974) found Ophiomorpha, a commonly observed shallow-water walled-burrow structure, associated
with a deep-water fauna containing the Nereites assemblages in the Upper
Cretaceous Point Loma Formation, San Diego (15.12, 15.13).

Rates of deposition and the process of substrate aggradation and
erosion was emphasized in a paper by Goldring (1964). Goldring's diagram
with comments by Frey (1971) is reproduced as Figure 7.1. Previous reference was made in the use of burrowing intensity to reconstruct rates of
sedimentation (Moore and Scruton, 1957). Intense burrowing destroying
stratification suggests slow sedimentation; slight or no burrowing high
rates (assuming oxygenated waters). A description of these relationships in
the Cretaceous of the Western Interior from Weimer (1973) and Weimer and
Land (1975) is presented as Tables 13.1 - 13.3 describing deltaic and interdeltaic shoreline sedimentation.

Burrowed to non-burrowed layers related to variation in rates of
sediment addition to the sediment interface is common in ancient marine
sandstones.

The use of trace fossils to determine water salinity in ancient
sequences has been reported by many authors. Not considering the effects
of rates of sedimentation, high burrow concentration means higher water
salinities; low burrow concentration may mean fresh water. These relationships have to be established in the modeling of genetic units in each ancient sequence. Associated lithologies, other faunas, inorganic structures,
etc., all must be considered before making a final determination on the
meaning of burrowing intensity. It is true that organisms that burrow for
a food supply are far more abundant in marine waters than in fresh waters.

For the Lower Cretaceous in the Western Interior, Siemers (1970) documented three trace fossil assemblages in a deltaic complex (Dakota Formation of Kansas) indicative of fresh, brackish and normal marine waters. A similar occurrence was noted by Weimer and Land (1972) for the Dakota Group in Colorado.

Summary

All geologists describing and interpreting sedimentary rocks should develop an acceptable level of proficiency in the use of biogenic sedimentary structures. One need not be an expert in Paleontology to derive useful data from trace fossils. When combined with data from inorganic structures and textures, the stratigrapher now has powerful tools to define process-controlled genetic units for use in facies analysis and the construction of stratigraphic models depicting ancient sequences.

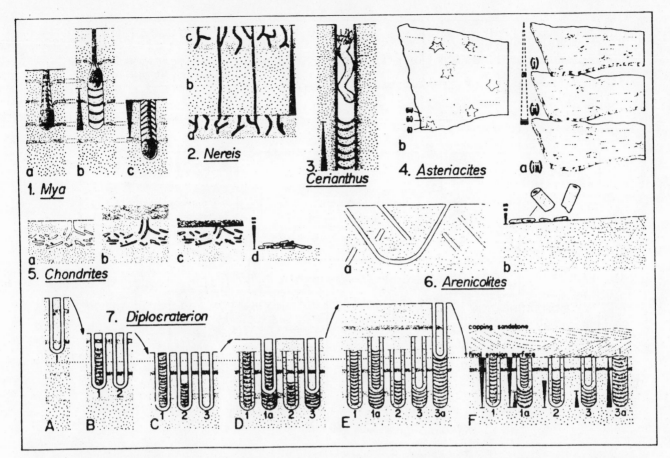

FIGURE 7.1 Amount of substrate aggradation or erosion (height of solid arrows) as reflected by subsequent adjustment in depth of burrowing by animals. (From Goldring, 1964, Fig. 1, by permission of Elsevier Publishing Company; compiled by Goldring from various sources.)

(1) Recent pelecypod burrows: (a) negligible deposition; growing animal burrows deeper. (b) rapid deposition; clam migrate upward, producing "sitz marks." (c) substrate scour; clam migrates downward.

(2) Recent polychaete burrows: negligible deposition (a) followed by rapid deposition (b) and then negligible deposition (c) Burrows in (a) and (c) mucus lined; "escape" burrows in (b) unlined, therefore less durable.

(3) Recent cerianthid burrow: animal moves upward with aggrading substrate.

(4) Fossil resting trace: animal moves upward with aggrading substrate (a), producing vertically superposed traces (b).

(5) Fossil burrows: feeding system (a) is filled in by different kind of sediment (b), followed by substrate scour (c) winnowing of sediment leaves lag concentrate of coherent burrow casts (d).

(6) Fossil burrows: substrate containing U-shaped burrows (a) is scoured partly away, leaving lag concentrate of fragmented burrow casts (b).

(7) Fossil burrows: burrow develops normally (A1), then is displaced downward with substrate scour (B1, C1-2), new burrow being constructed periodically (B2, C3); with renewed deposition some burrows are displaced upward (D1a, D3) and others are abandoned (D1-2); with rapid deposition, relatively more burrows are abandoned (E); at end of episode, all burrows are truncated and abandoned (F).

From Frey, 1971, modified after Goldring, 1964.

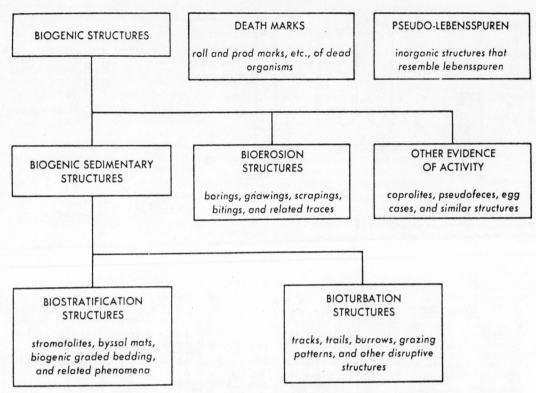

FIG. 7.2 Major relationships among biogenic structures and of these to other phenomena. (From Frey, 1971.)

Table 7.2 *Major areas of geology in which ichnological information is potentially useful* (condensed from Frey, 1971)

1. *paleontology*
   A. fossil record of soft-bodied animals
   B. evidence of activity by organisms
   C. diversity of fossil assemblages
   D. evolution of the metazoa and of behavior

2. *stratigraphy*
   A. biostratigraphy of "unfossiliferous" rocks
   B. correlation by marker beds
   C. structural attitude of beds
   D. structural deformation of sediments

3. *sedimentology*
   A. production of sediment by boring organisms
   B. alteration of grains by sediment-ingesting animals
   C. sediment reworking
      (1) destruction of initial fabrics and sedimentary structures
      (2) creation of new fabrics and sedimentary structures

4. *depositional environments and paleoecology*
   A. bathymetry
   B. temperature and salinity
   C. depositional history
      (1) rates of deposition
      (2) amounts of sediment deposited or eroded
   D. aeration of water and sediments
   E. substrate coherence and stability

5. *consolidation of sediments*
   A. initial history of lithification
   B. measures of compaction

DIFFERENTIATION OF BIOGENIC STRUCTURES

1. *biogenic structure*—in ichnology, tangible evidence of activity by an organism, fossil or recent, other than the production of body parts. Embraces the entire spectrum of substrate traces or structures that reflect a behavioral function: biogenic sedimentary structures, biocrosion structures, and other miscellaneous features representing activity. Excludes molds of "body fossils" that result from passive contact between body parts and the host substrate, but not imprints made by the body parts of active organisms.

    A. *biogenic sedimentary structure*—a biogenic structure produced by the activity of an organism upon or within an unconsolidated particulate substrate: bioturbation structures and biostratification structures.

        (1) *bioturbation structure*—a biogenic sedimentary structure that reflects the disruption of biogenic and physical stratification features or sediment fabrics by the activity of an organism: tracks, trails, burrows, and similar structures.

        (2) *biostratification structure*—a biogenic sedimentary structure consisting of stratification features imparted by the activity of an organism: biogenic graded bedding, byssal mats, certain stromatolites, and others.

    B. *biocrosion structure*—a biogenic structure excavated mechanically or biochemically by an organism into a rigid substrate: borings, gnawings, scrapings, bitings, and related traces.

DISCIPLINES AND COMPONENTS

2. *ichnology*—the overall study of traces made by organisms, including their description, classification, and interpretation. Divisions include *palichnology* (= *paleoichnology*) for fossil traces, and *neoichnology* for recent ones.

    A. *trace*—in ichnology, an individually distinctive biogenic structure, especially one that is related more or less directly to the morphology of the organism that made it: tracks, trails, burrows, borings, coprolites, fecal castings, and similar features, fossil or recent (= *lebensspur*). Excludes biostratification structures and other traces lacking diagnostic anatomical features.

    B. *ichnocoenose*—an assemblage of traces. Components include the *ichnofauna*, or animal traces, and the *ichnoflora*, or plant traces (such as algal borings).

    C. *trace fossil*—a fossil trace (= *ichnofossil*).

3. *ethology*—in ichnology, the study or interpretation of the behavior of organisms as reflected by their traces.

Table 7.4 *Useful descriptive-genetic terms*
(modified from Frey, 1971)

TRACKS AND TRAILS

track—an impression left in underlying sediment by an individual foot or podium.

trackway—a succession of tracks reflecting directed locomotion.

trail—a continuous groove produced during locomotion by an animal having part of its body in contact with the substrate surface, or a continuous subsurface trace made by an animal traveling from one point to another.

BURROWS

burrow—an excavation made within unconsolidated sediment. Excludes intrastratal trails.

burrow system—highly ramified and (or) interconnected burrows.

shaft—a dominantly vertical burrow, or a dominantly vertical component of a burrow system having prominent vertical and horizontal parts.

tunnel—a dominantly horizontal burrow, or a dominantly horizontal component of a burrow system having prominent vertical and horizontal parts (= *gallery*).

burrow lining—a thickened burrow wall constructed by organisms as a structural reinforcement. May consist of (1) host sediments retained essentially by mucus impregnation, (2) pelletoidal aggregates of sediment shoved into the wall, like mud-daubed chimneys, (3) detrital particles selected and cemented like masonry, or (4) leathery or felted tubes consisting mostly of chitinophosphatic secretions by organisms. Burrow linings of types 3 and 4 are commonly called *dwelling tubes*.

burrow cast—sediments infilling a burrow (= *burrow fill*). Sediment fill may be either *active*, if done by animals, or *passive*, if done by gravity. Active fill is termed *back fill* wherever U-in-U laminae, etc., show that the animal packed sediment behind itself as it moved through the substrate.

MISCELLANEOUS

configuration—in ichnology, the spatial relationships of lebensspuren, including the disposition of component parts and their orientation with respect to bedding and (or) azimuth.

spreite—a blade-like to sinuous, U-shaped, or spiraled structure consisting of sets or co-sets of closely justaposed, repetitious, parallel or concentric feeding or dwelling burrows or grazing traces; individual burrows or grooves comprising the spreite commonly anastomose into a single trunk or stem (as in *Daedalus*) or are strung between peripheral "support" stems (as in *Rhizocorallium*). *Retrusive* spreiten are extended upward, or proximal to the initial point of entry by the animal, and *protrusive* spreiten are extended downward, or distal to the point of entry.

Lebensspuren	Basic definition	Characteristic morphology	Examples*
resting traces (= cubichnia)	shallow depressions made by animals that temporarily settle onto, or dig into, the substrate surface.	bowl- or trough-like relief, recording to some extent the latero-ventral morphology of the animal; structures are typically isolated but may intergrade with crawling traces.	*Asteriacites Ichnocumulus Lockeia Rusophycus*
crawling traces (= repichnia)	trackways and trails (epistratal or intrastratal) made by animals traveling from one place to another.	successions of tracks, or elongated, continuous, linear or sinuous structures; some branched; commonly annulated; complete form may be preserved.	*Aulichnites Climactichnites Cruziana Scolicia*
grazing traces (= pascichnia)	grooves, pits, and furrows made mostly by mobile deposit-feeding animals, at or near the substrate surface.	unbranched, non-overlapping, curved to tightly coiled patterns, or delicately constructed spreiten; complex patterns reflect full utilization of space; complete form may be preserved.	*Helminthoida Nereites Paleodictyon Polykampton*
feeding structures (= fodinichnia)	more or less temporary burrows constructed by deposit-feeding animals; structures typically also provide shelter for the animals.	single, branched or unbranched, cylindrical to sinuous shafts or U-shaped burrows, or spreiten structures; oriented at various angles; complete form may be preserved.	*Chondrites Daedalus Phycodes Rosselia*
dwelling structures (= domichnia)	burrows or dwelling tubes providing more or less permanent domiciles, mostly for semisessile, suspension-feeding animals.	simple, bifurcated, or U-shaped structures perpendicular or inclined to bedding, or intricate burrow systems; complete form may be preserved.	*Cylindricum Gyrolithes Ophiomorpha Skolithos*

* See Häntzschel (1962) for illustrations.

GENERAL TERMS

toponomy—primarily, the description and classification of lebensspuren with respect to their mode of preservation and occurrence (position on or within a stratum, or relative to the casting medium), and secondarily, the interpretation of the mechanical origin of traces.

bioturbation—the reworking of sediments by an organism.

bioturbate texture—gross texture imparted to sediment by extensive bioturbation; typically consists of dense, contorted, or interpenetrating burrows or other traces, few of which are distinct morphologically. Where burrows are somewhat less crowded and are thus more distinct individually, the sediment is said to be *burrow mottled*.

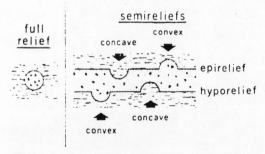

FIG. 7.2 Toponomic classification of bioturbation structures by A. Seilacher.

After Frey, 1974

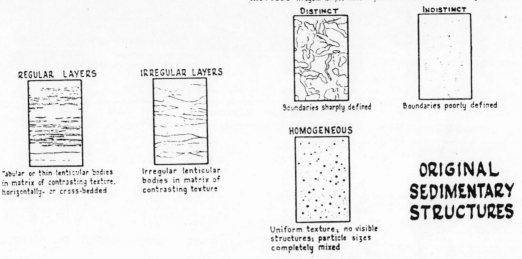

MOTTLES: Irregular lumps, tubes or pockets in matrix of contrasting texture

REGULAR LAYERS

Tabular or thin lenticular bodies in matrix of contrasting texture, horizontally- or cross-bedded

IRREGULAR LAYERS

Irregular lenticular bodies in matrix of contrasting texture

DISTINCT

Boundaries sharply defined

INDISTINCT

Boundaries poorly defined

HOMOGENEOUS

Uniform texture, no visible structures; particle sizes completely mixed

ORIGINAL SEDIMENTARY STRUCTURES

FIG. 7.3 Basic types of minor internal structures.

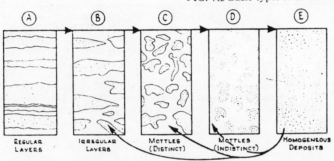

Ⓐ Ⓑ Ⓒ Ⓓ Ⓔ

REGULAR LAYERS — IRREGULAR LAYERS — MOTTLES (DISTINCT) — MOTTLES (INDISTINCT) — HOMOGENEOUS DEPOSITS

FIG. 7.4 -Progressive alteration of sediments by burrowing organisms. Sequences of minor internal structures formed by continuing action of burrowing animals. Top arrows indicate sequence formed by destruction of primary and secondary structures. Bottom arrows show how mottles or irregular layers may be created from homogeneous deposits.

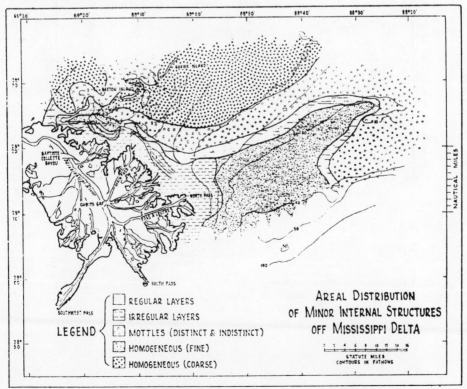

LEGEND
☐ REGULAR LAYERS
☐ IRREGULAR LAYERS
☐ MOTTLES (DISTINCT & INDISTINCT)
☐ HOMOGENEOUS (FINE)
☐ HOMOGENEOUS (COARSE)

AREAL DISTRIBUTION OF MINOR INTERNAL STRUCTURES OFF MISSISSIPPI DELTA

STATUTE MILES
CONTOURS IN FATHOMS

FIG. 7.5 Distributions of minor structures north and east of Mississippi Delta.

After Moore and Scruton, 1957

51

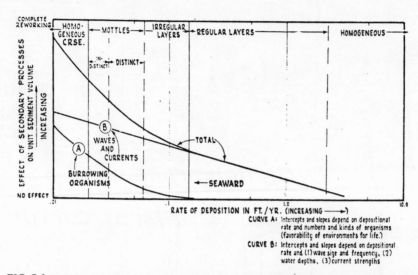

FIG. 7.6 Relations of minor internal structures to rate of deposition and processes off Mississippi Delta. Decreasing rate of deposition off Mississippi Delta causes effects of secondary processes to be greatest offshore in deeper water, although intensity of physical processes such as waves is greatest in shallow water nearshore.

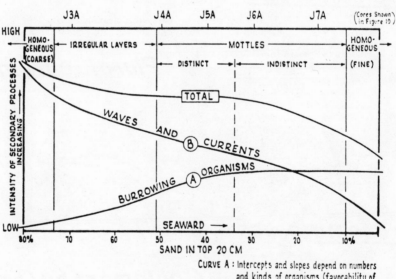

FIG. 7.7 Relations of minor structures, sources of sand, and process intensities in Gulf of Mexico off central Texas coast. Relatively constant depositional rate.

After Moore and Scruton, 1957

52

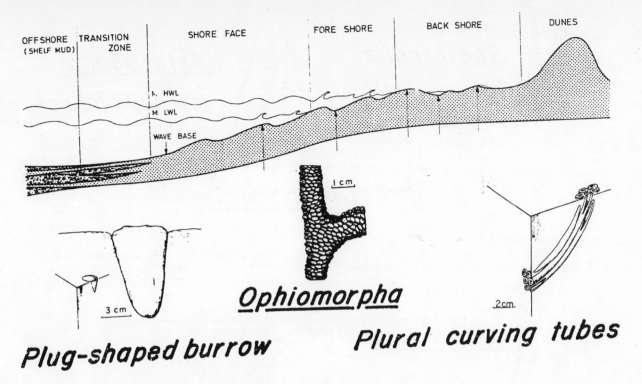

Ophiomorpha

Plug-shaped burrow

Plural curving tubes

FIG. 7.8 Upper shoreface, shoreface-foreshore transition and foreshore.

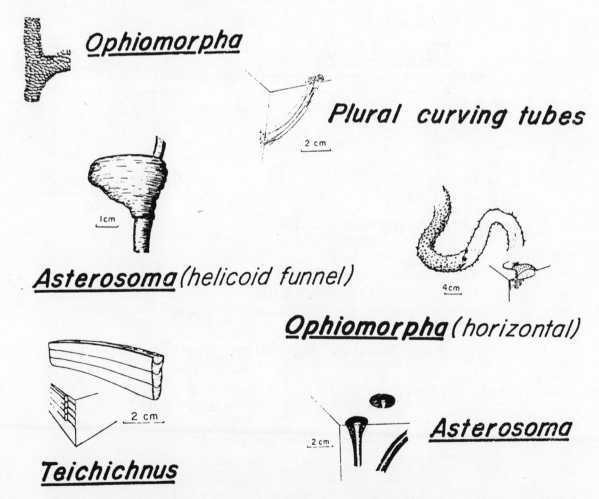

Ophiomorpha

Plural curving tubes

Asterosoma *(helicoid funnel)*

Ophiomorpha *(horizontal)*

Teichichnus

Asterosoma

FIG. 7.9 Lower Shoreface. This facies is characterized by fine- to medium-grained, dirty sand and an abundance of trace fossils. The vertical arrangement of trace fossils illustrated here represents the general vertical sequence of traces in the lower shoreface.

After Howard, 1972

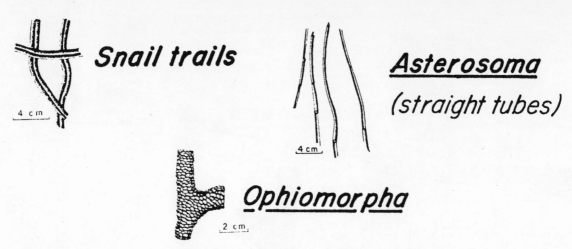

Snail trails

Asterosoma
(straight tubes)

Ophiomorpha

FIG. 7.10. Offshore-shoreface transition. This facies is characterized by thick beds of crossbedded fine sand. Burrowing is much less than in facies above and below. The trace fossils shown are generally the only forms and these are not abundant.

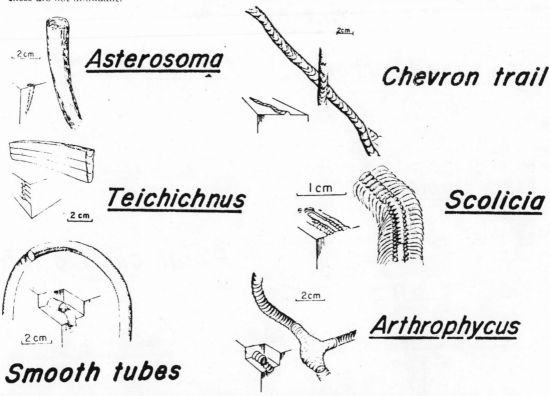

Asterosoma

Chevron trail

Teichichnus

Scolicia

Smooth tubes

Arthrophycus

FIG. 7.11. Offshore facies. This facies is composed of very thin-bedded, highly burrowed siltstone. The most abundant trace fossils are illustrated and they show no obvious preferred vertical segregation.

UPPER CRETACEOUS ICHNOFAUNAS FROM U.S.A.

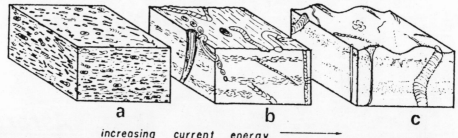

increasing current energy ⟶

FIG. 7.12. General facies present in Lower Campanian rocks of east-central Utah (Blackhawk Formation and Panther Sandstone Tongue, Star Point Formation); a highly burrow-mottled grey siltstones containing very few distinctive trace fossils, representing offshore deposition; b very fine-grained sandstones containing larger but less abundant burrow mottles and many distinctive trace fossils, representing nearshore deposition; c fine to medium grained sandstones containing little burrow mottling but numerous distinctive trace fossils, representing nearshore and shore deposition.

After Howard, 1972

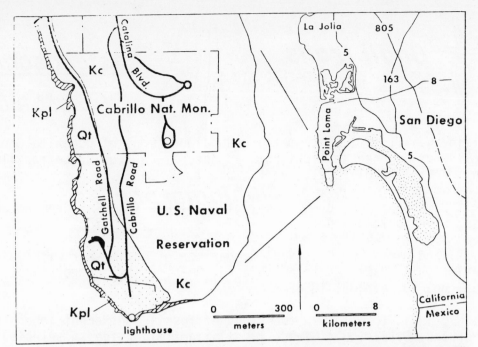

Figure 7.13 Location of study area is that part of Point Loma Formation (Kpl, diagonal lines) exposed in sea cliffs from the southern end of Point Loma northward along west side of peninsula to northern boundary of Cabrillo National Monument. Kc = Upper Cretaceous Cabrillo Formation; Qt (stipple) = Upper Pleistocene terrace deposits. Numbers identify interstate highways.

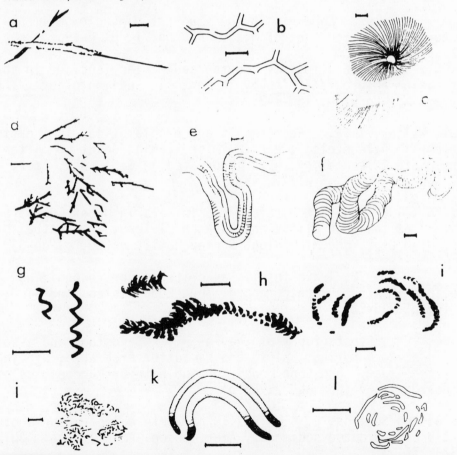

Figure 7.14 Trace fossils in Point Loma Formation. These traces occur parallel to bedding planes and are viewed from above. Bar is 2 cm long in all except b, in which it is 15 cm. (a) Typical pellet-lined *Ophiomorpha* and associated thin, straight, mud-filled burrows in sandstone. (b) *Thalassinoides* on upper surface of sandstone bed. (c) Flat *Zoophycos* in thin mudstone; spreite structure radiates from vertical central tube. (d) Large *Chondrites* in thin mudstone lamina. (e) Base of *Scolicia* exposed by erosion of mudstone from upper surface of sandstone bed. (f) Bedding-plane section through upper part of *Scolicia* in mudstone; feather-stitch structure left of center is at top of burrow. (g) *Belorhaphe* in mudstone. (h) Two specimens of *Nereites* in mudstone. (i) *Spirophycus* in mudstone. (j) Unidentified mud-filled burrows in mudstone. (k) Unidentified sand-filled burrow in mudstone. (l) Unidentified mud-filled burrows in mudstone.

After Kern and Warme, 1974

55

Chamberlain, C. K., 1971, Bathymetry and paleoecology of Ouachita Geo-
    syncline of southeastern Oklahoma as determined from trace fossils, Amer.
    Assoc. Petrol. Geol. Bull., v. 55, no. 1. p. 34-50.

Crimes, T. P. and Harper, J. C. (eds.) 1970, Trace fossils, Seel House
    Press, Liverpool, 547 p.

*Exum, F. A. and Harms, J. C., 1968, Comparison of marine-bar with valley-
    stratigraphic traps, Western Nebraska, Amer. Assoc. Petrol. Geol. Bull.,
    v. 52, no. 10, p. 1851-1868.

Frey, R. W., 1971, Ichnology - the study of fossil and Recent lebensspuren
    in Perkins, B. F. (ed.), Trace fossils, a field guide to selected
    localities in Pennsylvanian, Permian, Cretaceous, and Tertiary rocks of
    Texas, and related papers, Louisiana State Univ., School Geoscience,
    Misc. Publ. 71-1, p. 91-125.

_____, 1973, Concepts in the study of biogenic sedimentary
    structures, Jour. Sed. Petrology, v. 43, no. 1, p. 6-19.

Goldring, R., 1964, Trace-fossils and the sedimentary surface in shallow-
    water marine enivronments in Developments in Sedimentology, v. 1,
    Elsevier, New York, p. 136-143.

Hantzschel, Walter, 1962, Trace fossils and problematica, in Treatise on
    Invertebrate Paleontology, Part W, Miscellania, Joint Committee on
    Invertebrate Paleontology, R. C. Moore (ed.), Geol. Soc. Amer. and
    Univ. Kansas Press, p. W177-W245.

Howard, J. D., 1966, Characteristic trace fossils in Upper Cretaceous
    sandstone of the Book Cliffs and Wasatch Plateau, in Central Utah
    Coals, Utah Geol. and Mineralog. Survey Bull., v. 80, p. 34-53.

*_____, 1972, Trace fossils as criteria for recognizing
    shorelines in stratigraphic record, Soc. Econ. Paleo. and Min., Sp.
    Pub. 16, p. 215-225.

Land, C. B., 1972, Stratigraphy of the Fox Hills Sandstone and associated
    formations, Rock Springs uplift and Wamsutter arch area, Wyoming; A
    shoreline-estuary sandstone model for the Late Cretaceous, Colo. School
    of Mines Quat., v. 67, no. 2, 69 p.

*Moore, D. G. and Scruton, P. C., 1957, Minor internal structures of some
    recent unconsolidated sediments, Amer. Assoc. Petrol. Geol. Bull., v. 41,
    p. 2723-2751.

Osgood, R. G., Jr., 1970, Trace fossils of the Cincinnati area,
    Palaeontographica Americana, v. 6, no. 41, p. 281-444.

Schäfer, W., 1962, Aktuo-Paläontologie nach Studien in der Nordsee,
    Frankfurt-am-Main, Waldemar Kramer, 666 p.

*Seilacher, Adolf, 1964, Biogenic sedimentary structures in Approaches to Paleoecology, Imbrie, J. and Newell, N. (eds.), Wiley and Sons, New York, p. 296-316.

_____, 1967, Bathymetry of trace fossils, Mar. Geol., v. 5, p. 413-428.

Shinn, E. A., 1968, Burrowing in recent lime sediments of Florida and the Bahamas, Jour. Paleo., v. 42, p. 879-895.

Siemers, C. T., 1970, Facies distribution of trace fossils in a deltaic environmental complex: upper part of Dakota Formation (Upper Cretaceous) Central Kansas (abs), Program Geol. Soc. Amer. Ann. Meeting, Milwaukee, Wisconsin, p. 683-684.

Spoelhof, R. W., 1974, Pennsylvanian stratigraphy and tectonics in the Lime Creek - Molas Lake area, San Juan County, Colorado, Colo. Sch. of Mines PhD dissertation T-1511 (unpublished), 193 p.

Warme, J. E., 1967, Graded bedding in the Recent sediments of Mugu Lagoon, California, Jour. of Sed. Petrology, v. 37, p. 540-547.

Weimer, R. J., 1973, A guide to uppermost Cretaceous stratigraphy, Central Front Range, Colorado: deltaic sedimentation, growth faulting and early Laramide deformation, The Mountain Geologist, v. 10, no. 3, p. 53-97.

Weimer, R. J. and Hoyt, J. H., 1964, Callianassa major burrows, geologic indicators of littoral and shallow neritic environments, Jour. Paleo. v. 38, p. 761-767.

Weimer, R. J. and Land, C. B., 1972, Field guide to Dakota group (Cretaceous) stratigraphy, Golden-Morrison area, Colorado, The Mountain Geologist, v. 9, nos. 2-3, p. 241-267.

LECTURE 7
(8)

ENVIRONMENTS OF DEPOSITION

Introduction

Accurate reconstruction of the environment of deposition of petroleum-
producing sandstones provides the scientific basis for predicting extensions
of productive trends and new field occurrences in stratigraphic trap exploration. The same approach can be used by geologist involved in exploring
for coal and sedimentary uranium deposits.

In most producing basins, exploration for petroleum has gone through
several stages: first, drilling near seeps; second, drilling on anticlinal
structures; third, the drilling of fault or unconformity traps generally on
flanks of anticlines (combination traps); and, fourth, the drilling of
stratigraphic traps. At present, most onshore United States exploration
efforts are involved with the search for the subtle combination traps or
stratigraphic traps. These traps are infinitely more difficult to find
than the closed anticline. However, geophysics with coordinated subsurface
data provide the tools, although expensive, to explore for the combination
traps. The stratigrapher by reconstructing environments of deposition
and preparing stratigraphic facies models has developed the tools for the
exploration of stratigraphic traps. (Geophysics has not as yet become a
viable tool in stratigraphic exploration.)

In defining and solving stratigraphic exploration problems in sandstone reserviors, geologists are keenly aware that the areal distribution
of a producing unit is limited. He also knows that the geometry of a
sandstone body is controlled by environment of deposition in which it was
deposited. Therefore, if he is to become more successful in predicting
sandstone trends, he must continually improve his skills in making accurate environmental interpretations, especially in predicting the distribution of porosity and permeability within the body. Although establishing the trend for a producing sandstone is not always easy, the task of
forecasting the occurrence of a potential-producing sandstone, which has
not been observed in surface or subsurface data, is infinitely more difficult.
Yet, the future of exploration rests in the solution of this type of problem

by new ideas generated in the minds of geologists.

The explorationist is primarily concerned with finding reservoir rock, i.e. porous and permeable sandstone. The amount of porosity and permeability within a rock body is controlled by two important factors: 1) the energy of the environment under which the sediments were deposited; and, 2) the post-depositional changes within the rocks as a result of lithification. In the discussion that follows about environments, primary emphasis will be on factors that control primary porosity and permeability.

Definition

Many definitions of environment of deposition have been published and most emphasize the sedimentary environment as having certain processes operating within a defineable spatial framework. In an excellent review article on sand bodies and sedimentary environments, Potter (1967, p. 340) summarizes several commonly used definitions for environment. He advocates the following: "A sedimentary environment is defined by a set of values of physical and chemical variables that correspond to a geomorphic unit of stated size and shape. Examples are an alluvial fan, a tidal flat, a point bar, and a beach." The relations between geomorphic unit, processes and resultant deposit were diagramed as follows:

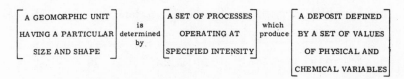

—Relations between geomorphic unit, processes, and resultant deposit.

An earlier and widely used definition by Krumbein and Sloss (1963, p. 234) defines a sedimentary environment as "the complex of physical, chemical and biological conditions under which a sediment accumulates." They stated that the elements and factors of the environment that must be evaluated are the materials, boundary conditions, energy and biological features.

Whichever definition is used one point is certain. The geologist reconstructing environments of deposition of ancient rocks works as geomorphologist of the past.

Classification

Knowledge of present-day sedimentary environments has expanded during
the past 20 years at an exponential rate. Because of man's requirements for
more energy, more and safer living space and more food supplies, researchers
throughout the world have examined the processes, sediments and the areal
distribution of modern environments. The results of the investigations have
given geologists new concepts and a more reliable scientific basis upon
which to interpret ancient sedimentary sequences. The geologic importance
of environment studies have been summarized in several new books (e.g.
Selley, 1970; Kukal, 1971; Reineck and Singh, 1973; Pettijohn, Potter and
Siever, 1973; Rigby and Hamblin, eds. [1972]). In addition many lengthy
papers have been published in an extremely diverse literature.

LeBlanc (1972) presented one of the more important papers on the
"Geometry of Sandstone Reservoirs" summarizing 30 years of experience
studying modern and ancient detrital sediments. The value of the paper
rests in the classification and description of environments and the emphasis placed on the distribution of porous and permeable sand in an overall
depositional framework. LeBlanc's classification (Figs. 8.1 - 8.3)
combines processes and geomorphic units into depositional models. This
classification is adopted in the following chapters and the reader is
urged to review Le Blanc's summary for each of the environments discussed.
Because of the excellence of Le Blanc's summary, there is no need to repeat
extensive descriptions for the environments. Therefore, major emphasis will
be placed on those aspects of environmental interpretation that are judged
to be most important in petroleum exploration of ancient sequences, especially in relation to the writer's own experience.

In addition to Le Blanc's classification, tables from the excellent
review article by Potter (1967) are included as Tables 1 - 6. These
tables give an environmental check list for factors to be considered in a
study of sand bodies and characteristics for the 5 more common sand bodies
(alluvial, tidal, turbidite, barrier island, marine shelf).

One aspect of applying the results of modern sediment studies to
the ancient record must be discussed. Some investigators have taken

stratigraphic models of the modern and Holocene record and attempted to make a 1 for 1 match with observations of sand bodies in ancient sequences. For example, the "Galveston Island barrier bar model" may be used exclusively as a standard reference for ancient regressive shoreline sands. In some cases it works, but in others, despite obvious differences, investigators have "shaped" their interpretation to fit the model. A more definitive and accurate approach is to develop a knowledge of the processes functioning within and associated with each modern environment and the resulting sediment accumulation. By recognizing a process-controlled genetic unit, building blocks may be established which permit reconstruction of large facies models. Each ancient sequence has its unique combination of variables in the interrelationship of processes. Observations of the ancient rocks must define the variables and provide the basis for determining their distribution in space and time. The Holocene stratigraphic facies models should serve only as a general guide.

In the following lectures, results of modern environment studies are described and key reference diagrams are reproduced. In the lecture outlines, only those points are listed which seem most important in interpreting ancient sequences. The references chosen are believed to be a representative sampling of the major processes controlling sedimentation.

The examples of ancient petroleum-producing sandstones are likewise believed to best illustrate the geology of known stratigraphic traps. By better understanding the origin of the reservoir rock of known fields, the explorationist has a better chance to discover and to develop efficiently the new fields which are so vital to society.

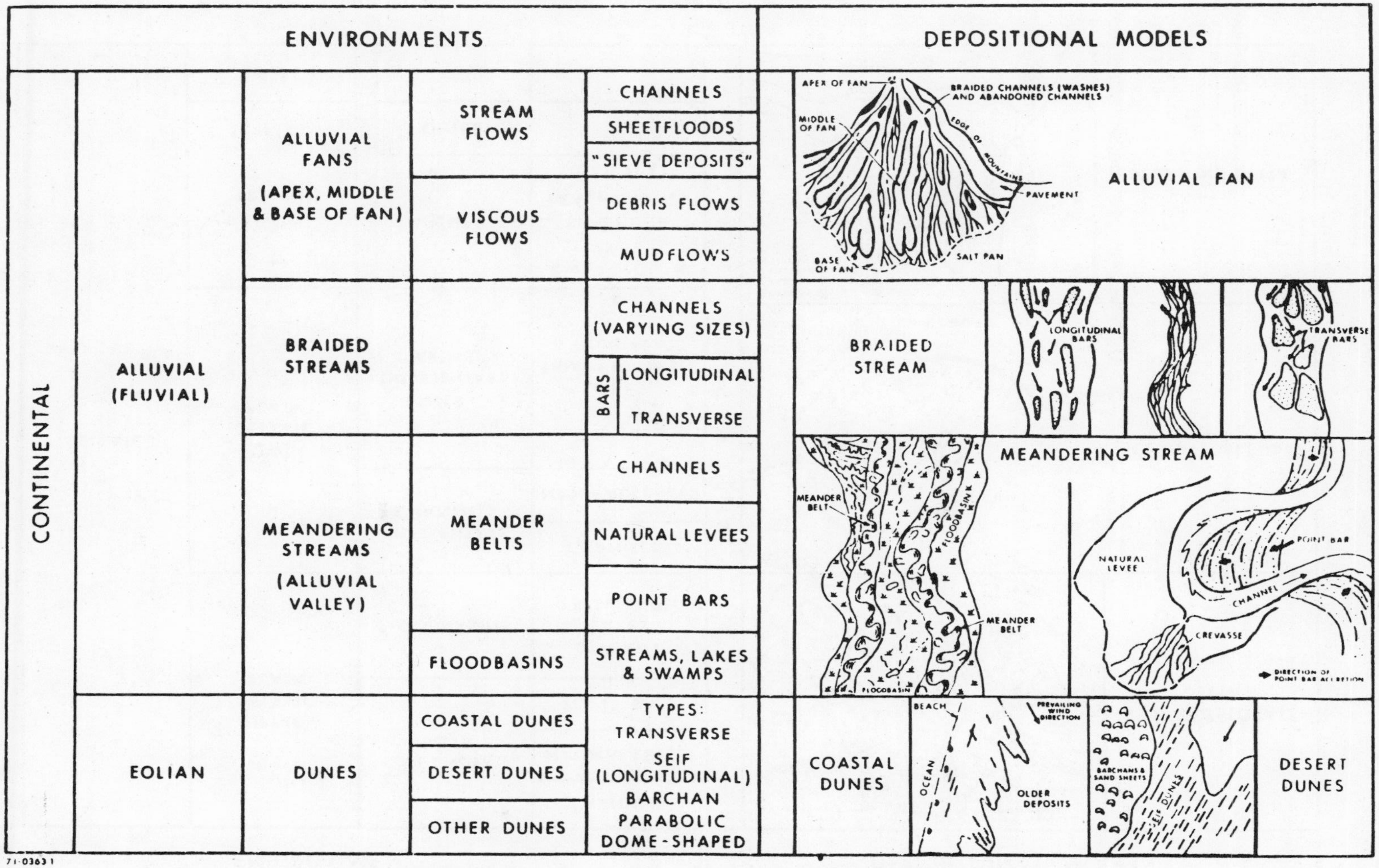

FIG. 8.1 Alluvial (fluvial) and eolian environments and models of clastic sedimentation.

From LeBlanc, 1972

63

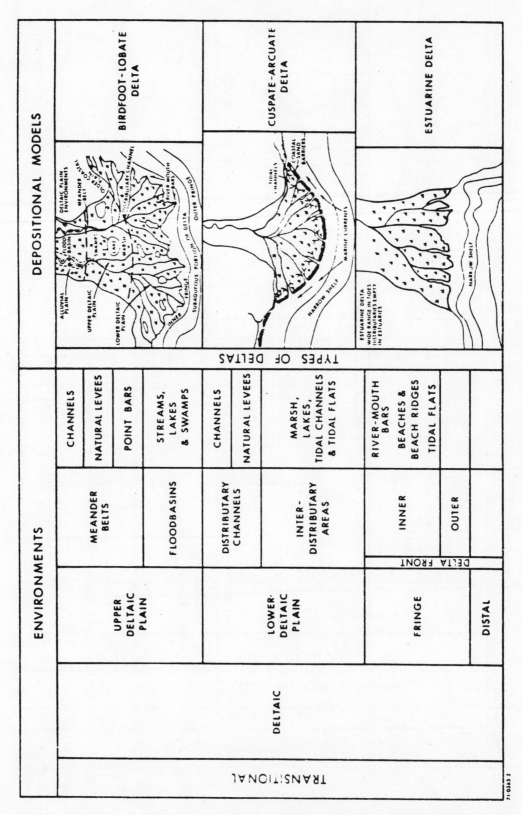

FIG. 8.2 Deltaic environments and models of clastic sedimentation.

From LeBlanc, 1972

64

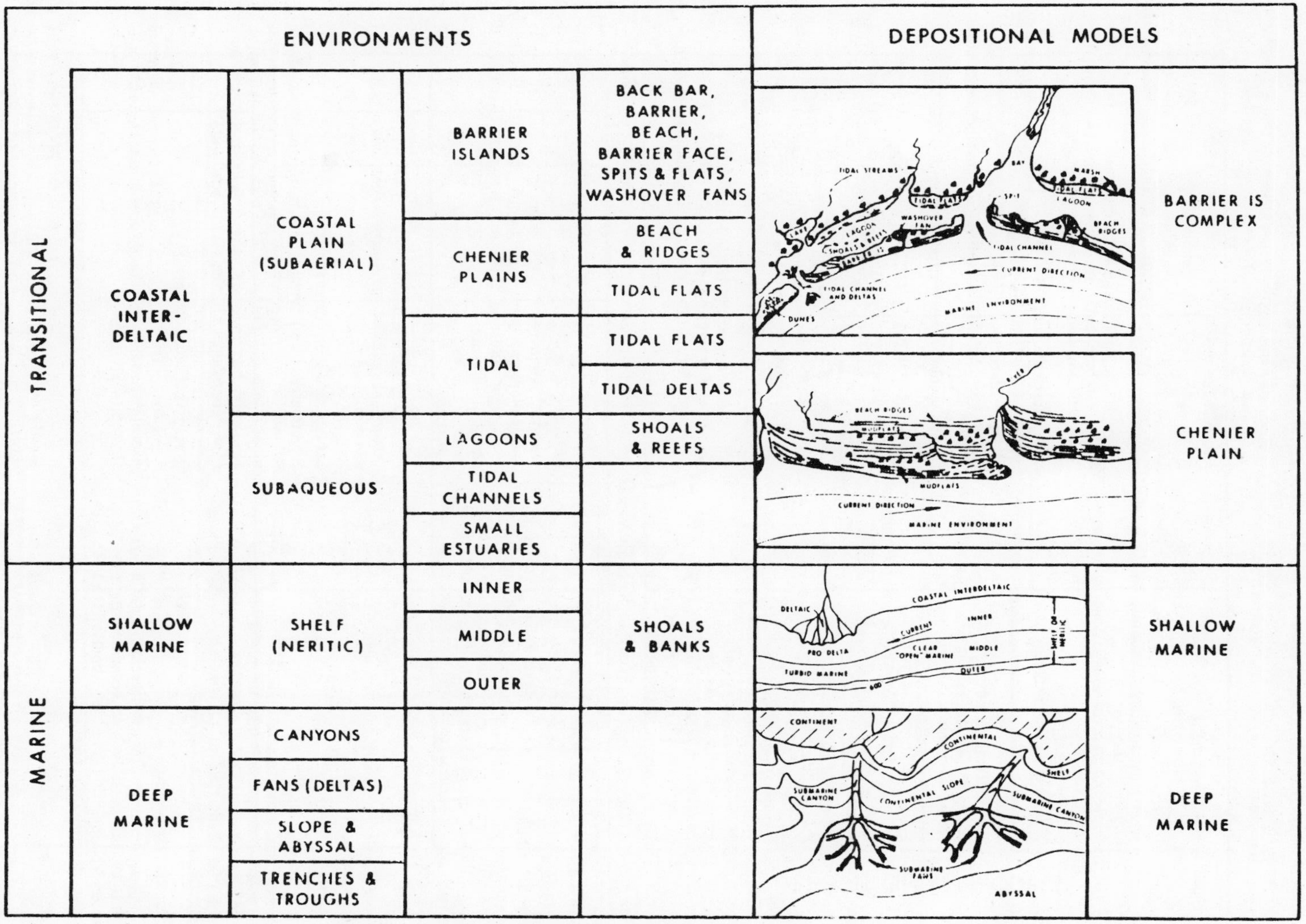

DEPOSITIONAL MODELS

ENVIRONMENTS

				Depositional Models
TRANSITIONAL	COASTAL INTER-DELTAIC	COASTAL PLAIN (SUBAÉRIAL)	BARRIER ISLANDS	BACK BAR, BARRIER, BEACH, BARRIER FACE, SPITS & FLATS, WASHOVER FANS	BARRIER IS COMPLEX
			CHENIER PLAINS	BEACH & RIDGES	CHENIER PLAIN
			TIDAL	TIDAL FLATS	
		SUBAQUEOUS		TIDAL FLATS	
			LAGOONS	TIDAL DELTAS	
			TIDAL CHANNELS	SHOALS & REEFS	
			SMALL ESTUARIES		
MARINE	SHALLOW MARINE	SHELF (NERITIC)	INNER	SHOALS & BANKS	SHALLOW MARINE
			MIDDLE		
			OUTER		DEEP MARINE
	DEEP MARINE	CANYONS			
		FANS (DELTAS)			
		SLOPE & ABYSSAL			
		TRENCHES & TROUGHS			

FIG. 8.3 Coastal-interdeltaic and marine environments and models of clastic sedimentation.

From LeBlanc, 1972

Table 8.1 Environmental Check List for Sand
Bodies

I. STRATIGRAPHIC
  A. Shape
    1. Elongate
      a. curved
        (1) meandering
        (2) dendritic
        (3) bifurcating
      b. straight
      c. relation to depositional strike
    2. Blankets (sheets)
  B. Lateral and vertical associations
    1. Continuous
      a. facies change
      b. oscillatory or cyclical
    2. Discontinuous
      a. unconformity
      b. structural cutoff
  C. Lithologic associations
    1. Range and abundance of rock types
    2. Lithofacies maps

II. PRIMARY SEDIMENTARY STRUCTURES AND BEDDING
  A. Inorganic structures
    1. Cross-bedding
    2. Ripple marks
    3. Parting lineation
    4. Sole markings
    5. Deformational structures
    6. Small-scale channels
    7. Shale chips and clay galls
  B. Burrows, tracks, and trails
  C. Character and organization of bedding
  D. Variability of directional structures
  E. Vertical sequence of bedding and structures

III. PETROGRAPHIC
  A. Mineralogy
    1. Primary
    2. Diagenetic
  B. Texture
    1. Grain-size parameters
    2. Shape and roundness
    3. Surface texture
    4. Fabric
      a. grain-to-grain contacts
      b. orientation of framework fraction
    5. Vertical sequence of textures

IV. PALEONTOLOGIC
  A. Autochthonous fossils
  B. Allochthonous fossils
  C. Specialized indicators of marine and non-marine
  D. Ecologic associations

V. GEOCHEMICAL
  A. Primary (Depositional)
    1. Minerals
    2. Isotopes
    3. Organic matter
    4. Trace elements
  B. Diagenetic (Secondary)
    1. Minerals
    2. Isotopes
    3. Organic matter, oil and gas
    4. Formation waters
    5. Structures: concretions, nodules, stylolites, *etc.*

Table 8.2 Characteristics of Alluvial Sand Bodies

(Alluvial–fan and bar–finger deposits not included)

PETROLOGY

Detrital. Abundant shale pebbles and shale–pebble conglomerates. Generally carbonaceous debris. Petrographically immature to moderately mature. Pebbles and cobbles, if present, may be both local and distal. Detrital plus chemical cements. Faunal content low to absent.

TEXTURE

Poor to moderate sorting and moderate to low grain-matrix ratio. Abundant silt in fine-end tail. Tendency to poor rounding. High variability.

SEDIMENTARY STRUCTURES

Asymmetrical ripple marks and abundant well-oriented cross-bedding, commonly unimodal. Parting lineation and deformational structures are common minor accessories. Beds tend to be lenticular with erosional scour. Some tracks and trails.

INTERNAL ORGANIZATION

Strong asymmetry. Upward decrease in grain size and bed thickness, possibly with conglomerate near base. Larger channel-fill sandstone bodies tend to be coarser-grained than smaller ones.

SIZE, SHAPE, AND ORIENTATION

Commonly very elongate. Width ranges from a few tens of feet to composites of 30 miles. Dendritic as well as anastomosing and bifurcating patterns. Elongate downdip. Excellent correlation of internal directional structures and elongation.

ASSOCIATED LITHOLOGIC TYPES

Vertical: overlying silty shales, commonly of alluvial origin. Possible peat and coal. Basal contact commonly sharply disconformable. Multistory sandstone bodies. Marine units in mixed sections. Lateral: silty shale and siltstone commonly with abundant carbonaceous material as well as roots, leaves, and stems. Multilateral sandstone bodies. Correlation generally difficult.

Table 8.3 Characteristics of Tidal Sand Bodies

PETROLOGY

Detrital. Argillaceous rock fragments, skeletal debris and collophane plus argillaceous material. Possibly some glauconite and authigenic feldspar. Detrital and chemical cements.

TEXTURE

Fair sorting, moderate to high grain-matrix ratio. Possibly shell conglomerate at base. Very similar to texture of alluvial sandstone. Peat, clay galls, and wood common.

SEDIMENTARY STRUCTURES

Asymmetrical and symmetrical ripple marks common. Abundant cross-bedding of variable thickness; commonly bimodal but may dip seaward or landward. Lenticular bedding dominant. Tracks, trails, and burrows abundant. Channels and washouts.

INTERNAL ORGANIZATION

Good asymmetry. Strong vertical decrease in grain size and bedding thickness, possibly with some conglomerate at base.

SIZE, SHAPE, AND ORIENTATION

A few tens of feet to more than 1,000 feet wide, mostly very elongate. Long axis at right angles to shoreline or parallel with estuarine axis. Straight to moderately meandering, dendritic patterns, the latter as tidal inlets. Also lunate bars in passes between barrier islands. Cross-bedding parallel with elongation; principal mode may point seaward as well as landward in estuaries.

ASSOCIATED LITHOLOGIC TYPES

Vertical: variable according to regressive or transgressive origin. Associated with interlaminated shale and sandstone of tidal origin and marine sediments. Disconformable basal contact. Lateral: interbedded siltstone and shale of tidal-flat origin, commonly with mollusks, worms, crustaceans, and possibly algae as well as marine sediments.

After Potter, 1967

Table 8.4 CHARACTERISTICS OF BARRIER-ISLAND SAND BODIES

PETROLOGY

Detrital. Heavy-mineral concentrates common. Skeletal debris, collophane, and minor glauconite. Conglomerates, if present, generally locally derived and may be mostly shells. Fauna are generally the more robust species. Mostly chemical cements.

TEXTURE

Commonly excellent sorting and very high grain-matrix ratio. Low variability of textural parameters between samples. Commonly good rounding.

SEDIMENTARY STRUCTURES

Asymmetrical ripple marks. Abundant gently inclined bedding. Lamination and lineation conspicuous on beach. Cross-bedding moderately abundant and may be eolian as well as water-laid. Variability of cross-bedding orientation, moderate to large. Bimodal distributions may occur on the beach. Burrows and channeling common.

INTERNAL ORGANIZATION

Sparse data indicate vertical increase in grain size and bed thickness, especially in regressive sequences.

SIZE, SHAPE, AND ORIENTATION

Widths from a few hundreds of feet to more than several miles. Thickness 20-60 feet. Very elongate, parallel with strand line. Sandstone bodies generally straight to gently curved. Grain fabrics and cross-bedding can be variable, especially if eolian transport important.

ASSOCIATED LITHOLOGIC TYPES

Vertical: variable according to regressive or transgressive origin. Basal contact generally fairly even and may be transitional. Lateral: separates marine from lagoonal or terrestrial deposits giving maximum lithologic contrast. Multilateral sandstone bodies common.

Table 8.5 CHARACTERISTICS OF MARINE-SHELF SAND BODIES

PETROLOGY

Detrital. Commonly few argillaceous fragments and micas. Conglomerates, if present, are locally derived. Authigenic feldspar and glauconite and some detrital carbonate may be present. Mostly chemical cements. Relict faunas are common at tops of sand.

TEXTURE

Good to excellent sorting and high grain-matrix ratio. Variability of textural parameters between samples is very low. Tendency toward good rounding.

SEDIMENTARY STRUCTURES

Symmetrical and asymmetrical ripple marks. Crossbeds may be abundant; orientation commonly variable and may be bimodal. Trails and burrows. Minor channels and washouts.

INTERNAL ORGANIZATION

Data sparse, but vertical trends in grain size and bedding thickness either may be irregular or may increase or decrease, according to possible transgressive or regressive origin.

SIZE, SHAPE, AND ORIENTATION

Size and shape, highly variable, ranging from irregular, small pods through elongate ribbons to widespread sheets of many miles. Bifurcating and dendritic patterns absent. Elongate bodies have variable orientation with respect to depositional strike: parallel, perpendicular, and random. Relation of cross-bedding orientation to elongation not well-known, but probably variable.

ASSOCIATED LITHOLOGIC TYPES

Vertical: variable according to regressive or transgressive origin, but mostly marine shale and (or) carbonates. Basal contact may be disconformable, but generally not of great magnitude. Lateral: generally relatively uniform silt-free shales or carbonates, commonly with rich and varied marine fauna.

Table 8.6 CHARACTERISTICS OF TURBIDITE SAND BODIES

PETROLOGY

Detrital. Rock fragments and immature minerals abundant as well as marine skeletals of both deepwater and shallow-water origin. Carbonaceous material generally present. Shale-pebble conglomerate. Cements are very largely detrital.

TEXTURE

Very poor to fair sorting and low grain-matrix ratio. Rhythmic alternation of beds produces abrupt juxtaposition of shale and sandstone. Rounding almost all inherited.

SEDIMENTARY STRUCTURES

Graded beds rhythmically interbedded with shale. Absence of large-scale cross-beds. Beds notable for their long lateral persistence. Sole marks, asymmetrical ripple marks, and laminated and convoluted beds are common. Trails and tracks are generally present.

INTERNAL ORGANIZATION

Few data. Grain size may be related to sand-body dimensions.

SIZE, SHAPE, AND ORIENTATION

Elongate sandstone bodies up to several miles; fairly straight but dendritic and bifurcating possible. Extend downdip into basin. Excellent correlation of directional structure and shape. But sheet and blanket-like deposits probably predominate. Large olistostromes not uncommon.

ASSOCIATED LITHOLOGIC TYPES

Vertical: commonly other marine shale and turbidite sandstone. Multistory sandstone bodies possible. Lateral: except for lower sandstone-shale ratio, notably little lithologic contrast. Mixed benthonic and pelagic faunas in shale and possibly reworked shelf faunas in sandstone.

After Potter, 1967

SEDIMENTARY ENVIRONMENTS

Amer. Assoc. of Petrol. Geol. Reprint Series 7 and 8: Sandstone reservoirs and stratigraphic concepts, I and II.

Krumbein, W. and Sloss, L. L. 1963, Stratigraphy and Sedimentation, W. H. Freeman and Sons, San Francisco.

Kukal, Z., 1971, Geology of recent sediments: Academic Press, New York, 490 p.

*LeBlanc, R. J., 1972, Geometry of sandstone bodies: in Underground Waste Management and Environment Implications, Amer. Assoc. Petrol. Geol. Memoir 18, p. 133-190.

Pettijohn, F. J., Potter, P. E. and Siever, R., 1973, Sand and sandstone Springer-Verlag, 618 p.

Potter, P. E., 1967, Sand bodies and sedimentary ervironments: A review, Amer. Assoc. Petrol. Geol. Bull., v. 51, p. 337-365.

Potter, P. E. and Pettijohn, F. J.,1963, Paleocurrents and basin analysis Academic Press, Inc. New York, 296 p.

Reineck, H. E. and Singh, I. B., 1973, Depositional sedimentary environments, Springer-Verlag, New York, 439 p.

*Rigby, J. K. and Hamblin, W. K. (eds.), Recognition of ancient sedimentary environments, Soc. Econ. Paleo. Min, Sp. Pub., no. 16, 340 p.

Selley, R. C., 1970, Ancient sedimentary environments, Cornell Univ. Press, Ithaca, N. Y.

Shelton, J. W., 1972, Models of sand and sandstone deposits, Okla. Geol. Sur. Bull. 118, 122 p.

Visher, G. S., 1965, Use of vertical profile in environmental reconstruction, Amer. Assoc. Petrol. Geol. Bull., v. 49, p. 41-61.

OUTLINE FOR LECTURE 8
(11)

DELTAIC ENVIRONMENTS

1. Major delta components:
    a) Definition and importance of recognition; delta as depocenter.
    b) Delta plain; receiving basin; shoreline (Figs. 11.1 - 11.3).
2. Classifications:
    a) Cuspate, (arcuate), lobate, elongate, (bird foot): based on shape
        of delta shoreline (or delta plain area) controlled by fluvial
        processes and sediment influx and energy of marine processes
        (waves and longshore currents) (Figs. 11.5, 11.6).
    b) High constructive vs high destructive deltas: based on effective-
        ness of marine processes acting on delta front (Fig. 11.7).
    c) Shoal water vs deep water: influenced by tectonics (subsidence)
        and rates of sedimentation.
3. Environments of deposition
    a) Delta plain: active (progradation) phase-Fig. 11.3. (dominantly
        fresh water): distributary channel, levee, back-levee swamps
        (well-drained, poorly drained), marshes, interdistributary
        troughs (bay or lake), crevasse (Figs. 11.8, 11.9).
    b) Delta plain: inactive (abandonment) phase-Fig.11.3 (dominantly
        brackish to marine): marginal basin (bay, lagoon or sound),
        marsh, swamp.
    c) Shoreline and subaqueous delta, Figs 11.3, 11.10, (basin portion of
        delta):
        Active phase: delta front, prodelta zone (Figs. 11.6, 11.10,
        11.11), distributary-mouth bar (proximal and distal portions),
        subaqueous levees, sand bars, spits, beaches.
        Inactive phase: barrier island, shore face, shelf.
4. Processes:
    a) Active vs inactive phases of sedimentation related to distributary
        channel flow and shifting depocenters.
    b) Deposition rates vs subsidence rates in combination with (a) above
        resulting in cyclic sedimentation (Figs. 1 - 4). Rd/Rs ratio; Rd=
        rates of deposition; Rs= rates of subsidence (Fig. 11.38).
    c) Distributary progradation of delta front--prodelta area because of

high rates of sedimentation (Figs. 11.6, 11.11B, 11.16 - 11.21). Lower rates in basin and on delta plain. High energy deposits rest on lower energy, therefore coarsening upward sequence.

d) Type of flow and mixing processes where river water and sediment enters basin and resulting sedimentation (Figs. 11.12 - 11.14).

e) Oversteepening of delta front slope resulting in slumping and sliding (lecture 6) because of high rates of sedimentation in shallow water.

f) Rates of lateral accretion (progradation) generally high compared to rates of vertical accumulation (Rd/Rs>1). Holocene deposits of major rivers show ratio of lateral to vertical accumulation of 5000 to 1 or greater; other relationships of rates of deposition to rates of subsidence; Rd/Rs = 1; Rd/Rs<1 (Fig. 11.38)

g) Role of levees and crevasse splays in sediment accumulation in delta plain (Fig. 11.7, 11.8).

h) Channel processes associated with active, partial abandonment, and abandoned phases (Figs. 11.22 - 11.25).

i) Biogenic processes--burrowing activity generally low; root zones common; high peat or organic muck accumulation on delta plain.

j) Destructive or modification action of marine processes on inactive portion of delta resulting in thin transgressive marine sheet sands.

k) Shifting depocenters in subsiding basin resulting in repetitive vertical shallow water sequences (cycles or cyclothems; Figs 11.1, 11.4, 11.18).

5. Genetic Units (facies--lithologic associations)

a) Highly variable because of complexity of processes.

b) General vertical sequences: claystone and mudstone (prodelta Table 13.2) overlain by sandstone (delta front - Table 13.1) overlain by lenticular carbonaceous mudstone and sandstone (delta plain-Table 13.4) (Figs. 11.2, 11.4, 11.6 - 11.11). Importance of carefully evaluating details of all 3 major facies in reconstructing ancient deltas (Lecture 13).

c) Common reservoir rocks in deltaic framework:

1) Distributary channel sand (delta plain) narrow, long, linear bars or sometimes with isolated pods of porosity and permeability along trend (Figs. 11.8, 11.22 - 11.25, Tables 11.1, 11.2).

Fining upward sequence.

   2) Bar finger (channel) sand (special type of above), Figs. 11.10
      - 11.11a. Narrow, long linear bars with excessive thickness
      due to subsidence during sedimentation related to compaction,
      diapirism, or growth faulting (Fig. 11.11a). Note mod-
      ification of isopachs from Fisk pattern (Fig 11.11).

   3) Distributary mouth (channel mouth) bar (figs. 11.10, 11.16,
      11.17); proximal and distal portions. (coarsening upward
      sequence). Tabular sand unit with variable geometry and
      lithology.

   4) Delta front or delta fringe sheet sand, Fig. 11.8a, (coalesc-
      ing distributary mouth bars--sand being deposited during
      active delta progradation) (coarsening upward sequence)

   5) Shoreline sands (barrier or chenier) and associated shelf
      sheet sands: sands formed during inactive delta phase by
      reworking of older deposits. Summarized in lectures 12 - 14.

   d) Associated facies:
      Deltaic vs non-deltaic facies are summarized in lecture 13,
      especially details of coastal plain, shoreline and shallow
      neritic lithologic associations.

6. Tectonics and Sedimentation
   a) For large depocenters (major rivers with high sediment yield),
      penecontemporaneous deformation and its influence on sedimentation
      is highly significant.
   b) Intimate association of deltaic sedimentation and growth faulting
      (listric normal type). Figs. 11.36 - 11.39.
      1) Rapidly deposited prodelta shales masses which upon burial
         retain pore water; described as undercompacted, low density
         high pressure, low velocity masses (Fig. 16.16, 16.17).
      2) Loading of shale masses because of progradation of delta front
         --distributary sands may cause diapiric movement of shale, or
         growth faulting, or both.
   c) Growth faults extending to basement controlling sedimentation by
      movement of major crustal blocks (Fig. 11.32).
   d) Interrelationship of rates of subsidence, rates of sedimentation
      and intrabasin deformation. Additional discussion of processes in
      Lecture 16.

71

7. Importance of deltaic sequences in petroleum exploration: probably contain most significant reservoirs in detrital sequences.

   a) Isolated sand bodies rapidly buried by clays and silts--most favorable; clear water delta--sand only, much less favorable because of lack of early trap.

   b) High organic content dumped by rivers and converted to petroleum after burial; intertonguing of reservoir rock with source rock.

   c) Closed fluid systems.

   d) Highly favorable conditions for development of stratigraphic traps; early migration and entrapment; prime prospective areas in depositional basin if geologic history favors preservation of trap.

8. Importance of deltaic sequences in coal exploration.

   a) Occurrences are similar to coal in fluvial sequences, i.e. back levee swamps and interchannel basin areas; also fresh water marsh and saline marsh and swamp (mangrove) are areas of peat accumulation, Fig. 11.9.

   b) Growth fault systems cutting swamps and marshes may be responsible for unusual thickness of peat on downthrown side of fault or in graben fault blocks. Thinner accumulations occur over upthrown or horst blocks. This extra accumulation of peat upon compaction may mean the difference between commercial and non-commercial coal. Growth fault systems with examples of their influence on coal in the Laramie Formation (Upper Cretaceous, Colorado) will be discussed in lecture 16.

   c) Associated facies with coal are channel sand, levee, silt and clay, underclay, ironstone and limestone (Fig. 11.4). They are related to chemical and physical processes of the channel, channel margin and rise and fall of groundwater table (Fig. 9.5a). Root zones are present under coal.

   d) Besides the in-situ coal described above, detrital coals are common in deltaic invironments, especially in interdistributary troughs (no root zones under this type of accumulation and no underclay).

9. Importance of deltaic sequences in uranium exploration.

   a) Similar to occurrences in fluvial sequences but most important target is the distributary channel sequence.

b) Oxidizing and leaching conditions on levee and in poorly drained swamp are in close proximity to reservoir rock (active fill) and reducing condition of inactive channel fill in which carbonaceous material is preserved during partial abandonment or abandoned phase. (Figs. 11.23 - 11.25, Tables 11.1, 11.2).

c) Thin channels in crevasse splay subdelta may also be important host rock because of proximity of porous and permeable sand to alternating oxidizing and reducing conditions.

10. Examples of ancient petroleum--producing sequences:

a) Cenozoic of Gulf Coast (deltaic depocenters and growth fault traps; main producing reservoir=neritic shelf facies. (Figs. 11.29 - 11.35).

b) Lower Cretaceous of Rocky Mountains: Peoria Field, distributary channel sandstone in stratigraphic trap. (Fig. 11.28).

11. Examples of deltaic sandstones available for study during seminar: Outcrop--"j" Sandstone (distributary channel, Lower Cretaceous); Fox Hills Sandstone (delta front and distributary channel, Upper Cretaceous); Cores--"J" Sandstone (Peoria Field, distributary channel); (Wattenberg Field, delta front).

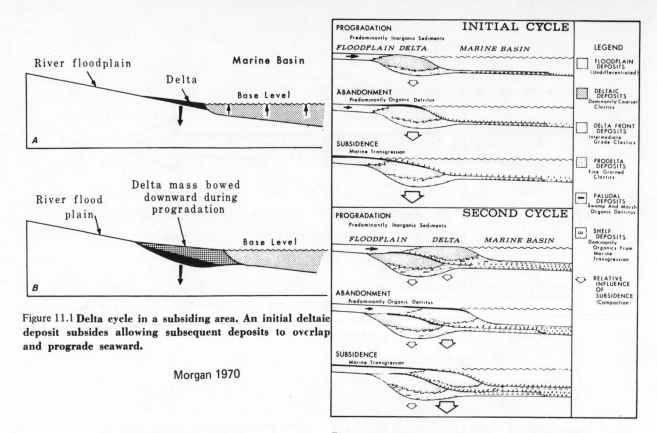

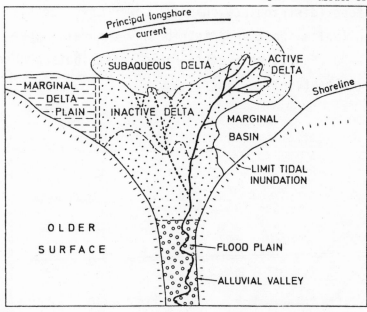

Figure 11.1 **Delta cycle in a subsiding area. An initial deltaic deposit subsides allowing subsequent deposits to overlap and prograde seaward.**

Morgan 1970

Figure 11.2 **Model of the delta cycle in a subsiding area.**

FIG. 11.3 Major physiographic components of a delta (Modified from Gagliano and McIntire, 1968, Fig. 1)

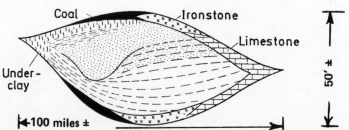

FIG. 11.4 Diagrammatic cross section of an idealized alluvial-deltaic cycle (Modified from Ferm and Williams, 1963, p. 356)

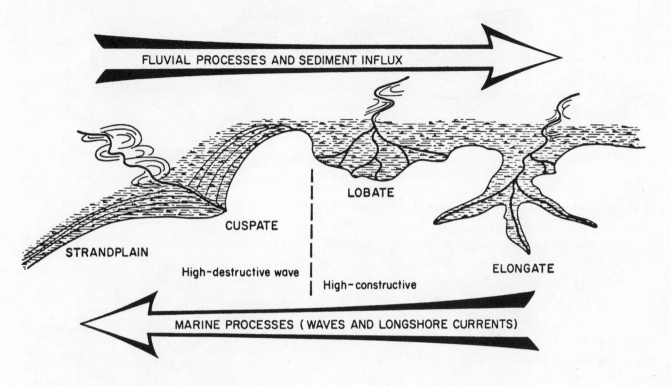

FLUVIAL PROCESSES AND SEDIMENT INFLUX

LOBATE

CUSPATE

STRANDPLAIN

ELONGATE

High-destructive wave

High-constructive

MARINE PROCESSES (WAVES AND LONGSHORE CURRENTS)

Arrows point in direction of increasing influence

FIG. 11.5 Relationship of marine processes and fluvial influence on wave-dominated deltaic coastlines. By A. J. Scott.

After Fisher, et al., 1969

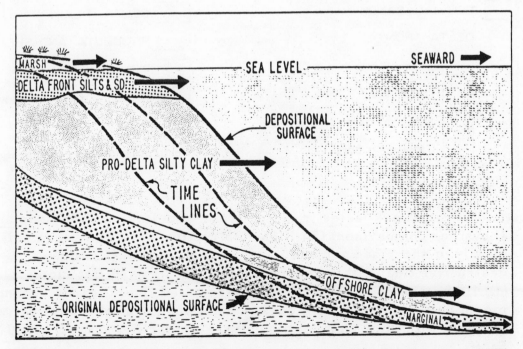

MARSH

DELTA FRONT SILTS & SD.

SEA LEVEL

SEAWARD

DEPOSITIONAL SURFACE

PRO-DELTA SILTY CLAY

TIME LINES

OFFSHORE CLAY

ORIGINAL DEPOSITIONAL SURFACE

MARGINAL

FIG. 11.6 Seaward migration of depositional environments in high-constructive deltas. From Scruton (1960).

75

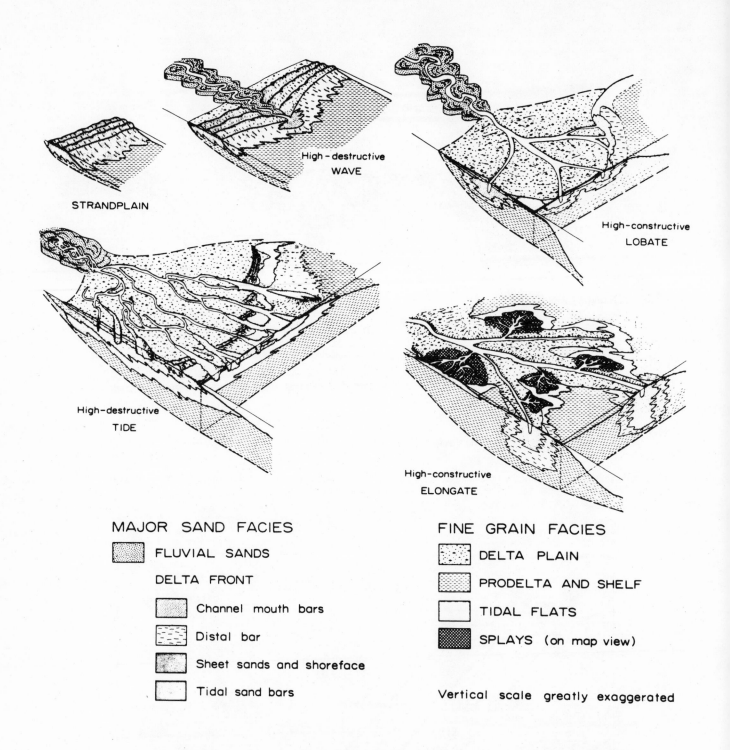

FIG. 11.7 Framework facies in major types of deltas. (A) Strandplain, shown for comparison; (B) High-destructive wave composed primarily of shoreface and associated fluvial sands; (C) High-destructive tidal with extensive tidal shoal or sand flat facies; (D) High-constructive lobate with associated fluvial sands, channel mouth bars and delta front sheet sands; and (E) High-constructive elongate with thick channel mouth bars or bar fingers. By A. J. Scott.

After Fisher, et al., 1969

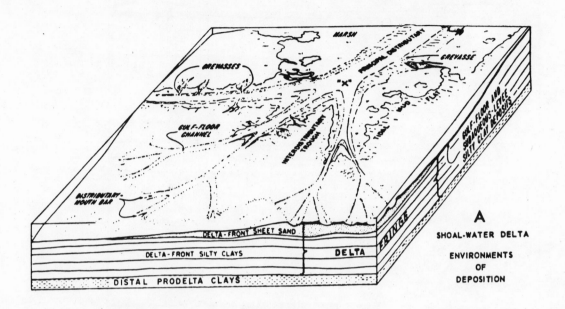

A

SHOAL-WATER DELTA

ENVIRONMENTS
OF
DEPOSITION

"X" - REFERENCE POINT

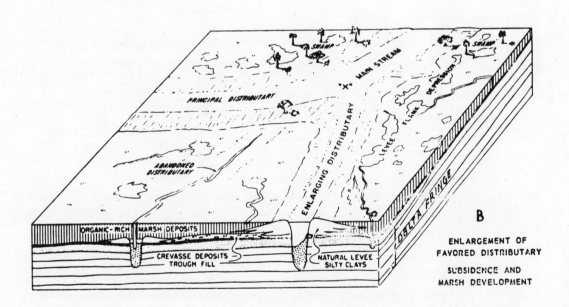

B

ENLARGEMENT OF
FAVORED DISTRIBUTARY

SUBSIDENCE AND
MARSH DEVELOPMENT

MODIFIED AFTER FISK, 1960

Figure 11.8 Block diagrams illustrating the development of a deltaic sequence resulting from the progradation of Mississippi distributaries, related environments and sediments. Modified after Fisk (1960).

After Fisher, et al., 1969

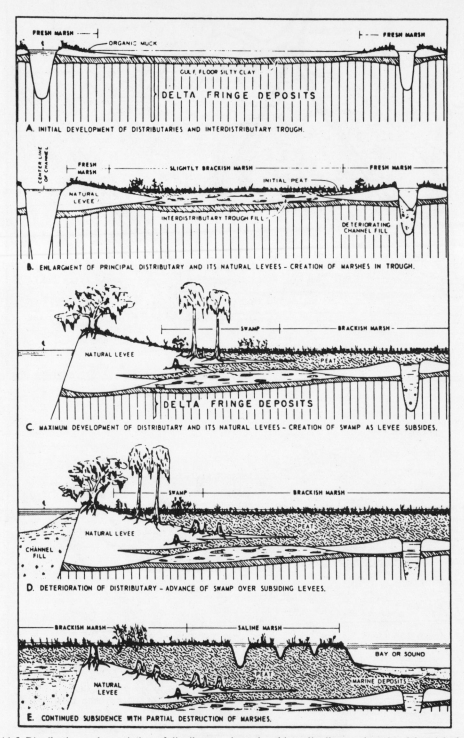

FIG. 11.9 Distribution and association of distributary channel and interdistributary deposits, delta plain facies, Mississippi delta system. Note well developed levee and associated organic deposits flanking channels and the fining upward sequence in the channel fill. From Bernard and LeBlanc (1965), modified from Fisk (1960).

After Fisher, et al., 1969

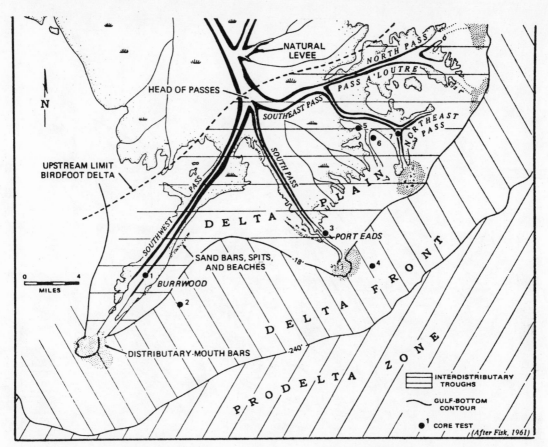

FIG. 11.10 Depositional environments of Mississippi birdfoot delta.

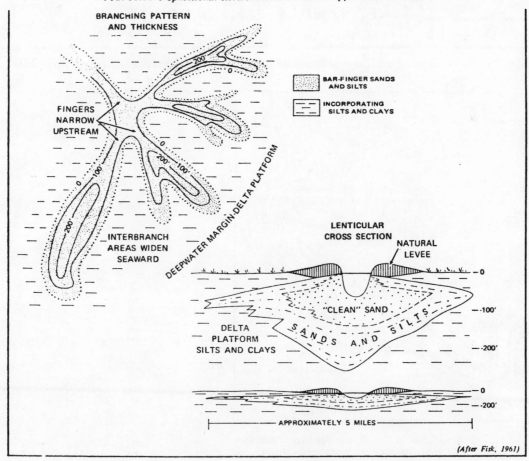

FIG. 11.11 Distinguishing geometric and sedimentary characteristics of bar-finger sands.

After Gould, 1970

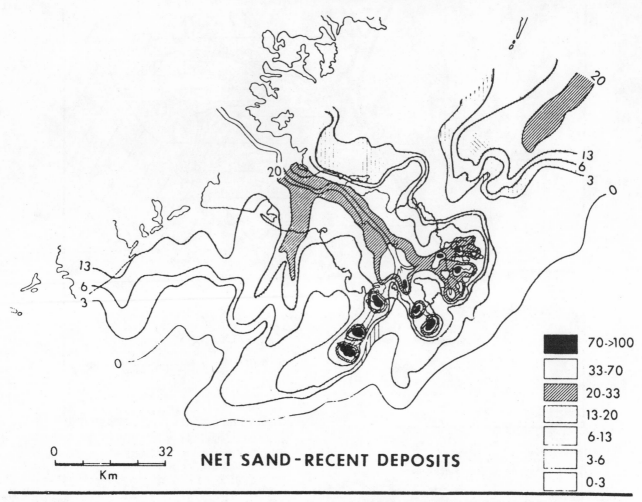

NET SAND-RECENT DEPOSITS

■	70->100
□	33-70
▨	20-33
□	13-20
□	6-13
□	3-6
□	0-3

0 ———— 32
Km

FIG. 11.11a Net sand thickness distribution pattern within the Recent deposits of the Mississippi River delta.

After Coleman, et al., 1974

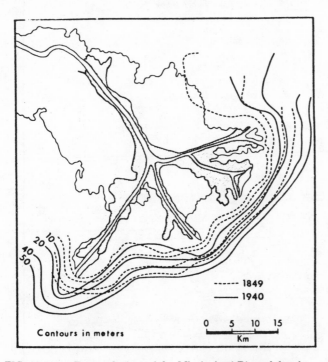

- - - - - 1849
———— 1940

Contours in meters

0 5 10 15
Km

FIG. 11.11b Progradation of the Mississippi River delta during the period 1869-1940. Offshore contours are in meters.

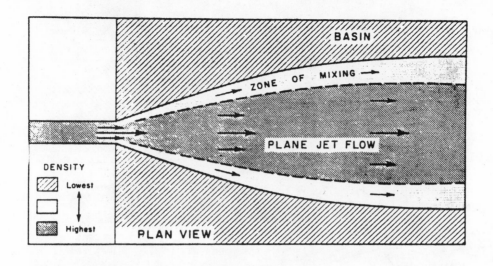

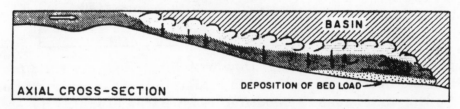

FIG. 11.12 Hyperpycnal flow. A plane jet in which the inflowing fluid is more dense than the reservoir fluid. This is the situation prevalent in turbidity flows. Modified from Bates (1953). By A. J. Scott.

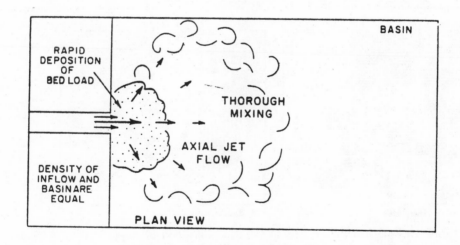

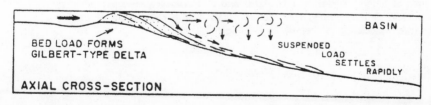

FIG. 11.13 Homopycnal flow. Axial jet flow in which the inflow and reservoir fluids have the same density. Rapid mixing associated with this type of inflow results in deposition of Gilbert-type deltas. Modified from Bates (1953). By A. J. Scott.

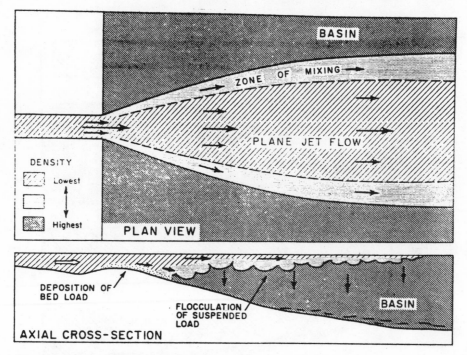

FIG. 11.14 Hypopycnal flow. Plane jet flow with the reservoir fluid more dense than the inflowing fluid. This situation is characteristic of rivers flowing into oceans. Modified from Bates (1953). By A. J. Scott.

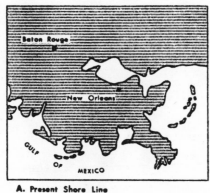

A. Present Shore Line

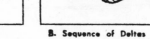

B. Sequence of Deltas

Figure 11.15 Alluvial plain in coastal Louisiana consisting of seven imbricating deltas formed in last 5000 years. Numbers denote sequence of ages of individual deltas; 1 is oldest and 7 is youngest, representing the present delta. Adapted from Scruton (1960) with permission of the American Association of Petroleum Geologists.

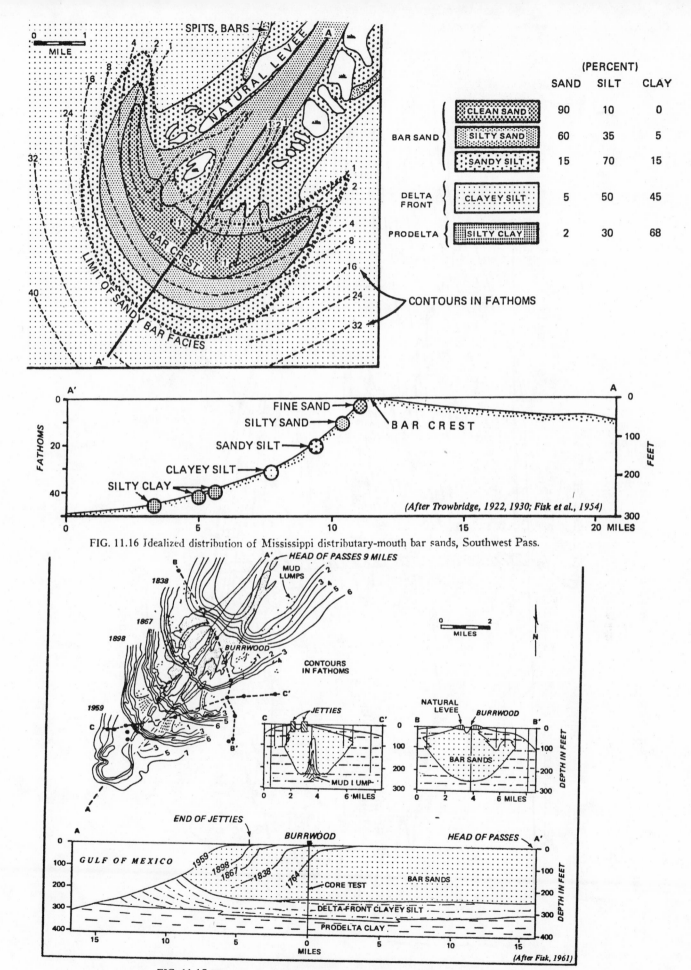

		(PERCENT)		
		SAND	SILT	CLAY
	CLEAN SAND	90	10	0
BAR SAND	SILTY SAND	60	35	5
	SANDY SILT	15	70	15
DELTA FRONT	CLAYEY SILT	5	50	45
PRODELTA	SILTY CLAY	2	30	68

CONTOURS IN FATHOMS

FIG. 11.16 Idealized distribution of Mississippi distributary-mouth bar sands, Southwest Pass.

(After Trowbridge, 1922, 1930; Fisk et al., 1954)

FIG. 11.17 Historic development of Southwest Pass bar finger.

(After Fisk, 1961)

83

After Gould, 1970

Overlapping cycles in a hypothetical delta complex.

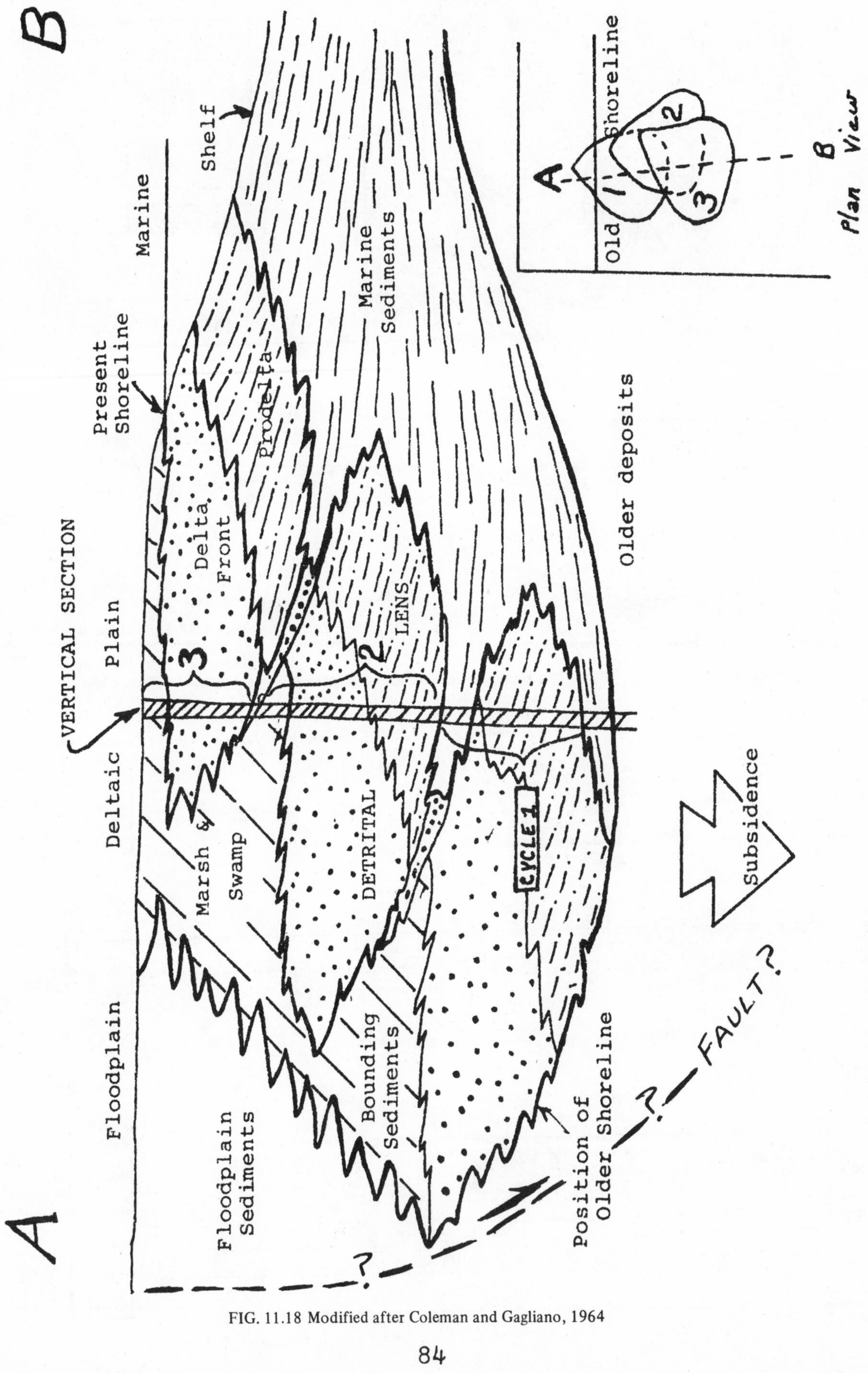

FIG. 11.18 Modified after Coleman and Gagliano, 1964

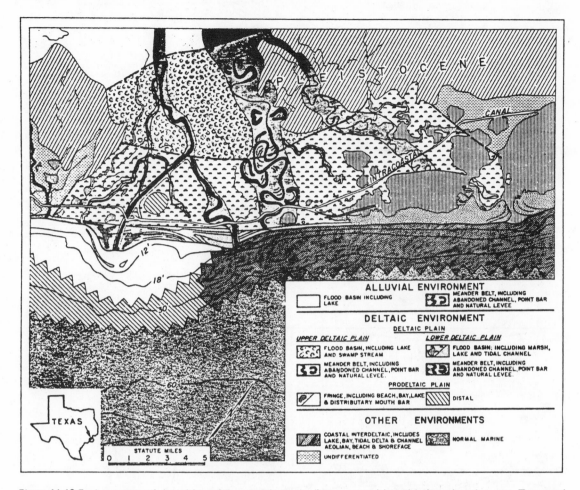

Figure 11.19 Environments of deposition of Brazos delta and adjacent coastal interdeltaic and marine area. Truncated Oyster Creek delta and "old" Brazos delta are northeast of "new" delta. Sand of "new" delta is present in subaerial part (lower deltaic plain) of "new" delta and subaqueous delta fringe. *From* Bernard and others (1970, fig. 30).

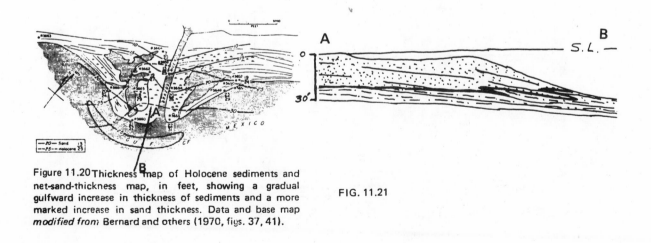

Figure 11.20 Thickness map of Holocene sediments and net-sand-thickness map, in feet, showing a gradual gulfward increase in thickness of sediments and a more marked increase in sand thickness. Data and base map *modified from* Bernard and others (1970, figs. 37, 41).

FIG. 11.21

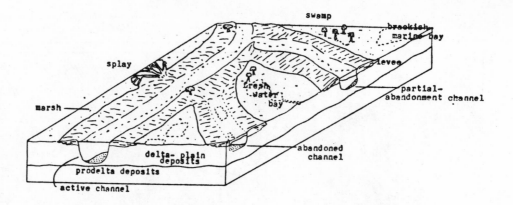

Figure 11.22 Block Diagram Showing Genetic Units Within a Delta Plain Environment
(modified after Meckel, 1972)

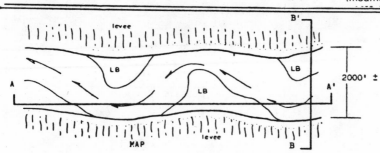

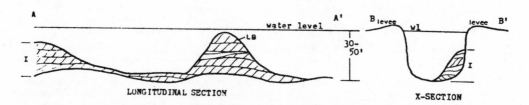

LONGITUDINAL SECTION   X-SECTION

Figure 11.23 Diagramatic Sections Showing Active-Channel Fill ( ). Lithologies are
medium to very fine-grained sandstone, thick planar- to trough-
cross-stratified, with possible scour base. LB = lateral bar.

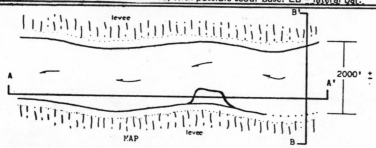

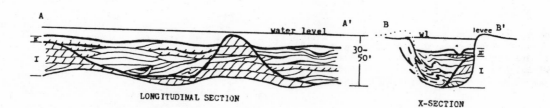

LONGITUDINAL SECTION   X-SECTION

Figure 11.24 Diagramatic Sections Showing Partial-Abandonment Fill ( ). Lithologies
are very-to fine-grained sandstone and interlaminated sandy siltstone,
thin-bedded to ripple-laminated, with occasional large-scale slumps.   is
active channel fill deposit (fig. 7).

After MacMillan, 1974

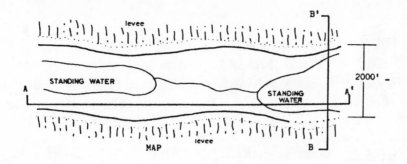

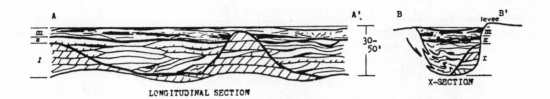

LONGITUDINAL SECTION

X-SECTION

Figure 11.25 Diagramatic Section Showing Abandoned Channel fill ( ). Lithologies
are very fine-grained sandstone, siltstone and claystone, interlaminated
to thinly bedded, with minor convolute—bedding. is active channel fill
deposit (fig.7); is partial abandonment fill deposit (fig. 14).

Table 11.1 Summary of Diagnostic Characteristics of Channel-Fill Facies

	Active-Channel Fill	Partial-Abandonment Fill	Abandoned-Channel Fill
Lithology	med to fg sandstone, possible rnded clayclasts and log imprints	f to vfg sandstone and inter-lam sandy siltstone, possible sub-rnded to ang clayclasts	vfg sandstone, siltstone, and claystone, interlam to inter-bedded
Sedimentary Structures: A. Inorganic	thin to dominantly thick-bdded, planar to trough cross-strat, possible scour base	dominantly thin-bdded, planar to trough cross-strat and finely lam siltstone drapes, minor slumpage and convolute bdding	thin bdded to thinly lam, break-up structures of ang unoriented clasts, slumpage and convolute bdding, possible desiccation cracks
B. Organic	transported organic material	transported organic material	possible root burrows at top of unit
Trace Fossils	occasional Teredo-borings in logs	none observed	none observed

Table 11.2 Summary of Diagnostic Characteristics of Channel-Margin Facies

	splay	levee	fresh-water bay	brackish--marine bay
Lithology	f to vfg sandstone, possible clasts of siltstone and clay-stone, scour base	sandy siltstone and claystone, lam vfg sandstone	carbonaceous, siltstone and claystones, inter-lam vfg sandstone, thin, white, kaolinite layers	intermixed vfg sandstone, siltstone, claystone
Sedimentary Structures: A. Inorganic	dominantly ripple-lam with possible trough to planar cross-strat at scour base	finely lam, usually disrupted by root burrows	vf lam to thin bdded, sub-parallel strat common	commonly destroyed by bioturbation
B. Organic	possible root burrows (fresh water) at top of unit	thin, laterally exten-sive root burrows	possible root burrows and carbonized imprints of leaves, twigs	commonly destroyed by bioturbation
Trace Fossils	none observed	occasional horiz burrows	possible horiz burrows 0.1-0.2 in. in dia.	horiz burrows, Siphonites, vert U-shaped burrows, non-discrete burrows

87   After MacMillan, 1974

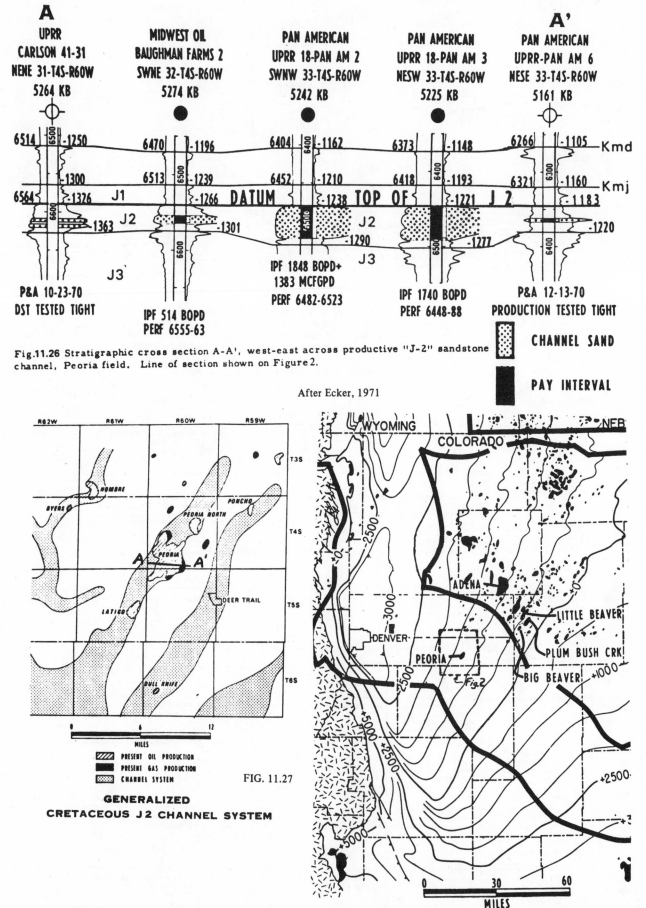

Fig.11.26 Stratigraphic cross section A-A', west-east across productive "J-2" sandstone channel, Peoria field.   Line of section shown on Figure 2.

CHANNEL SAND

PAY INTERVAL

After Ecker, 1971

GENERALIZED
CRETACEOUS J2 CHANNEL SYSTEM

FIG. 11.27

Fig. 11.28 Index map of Denver-Julesburg basin, showing location of Peoria field and boundary of Union Pacific Railroad land grant.   Structural contours are on top of Cretaceous "J" sandstone.

After Ecker, 1971

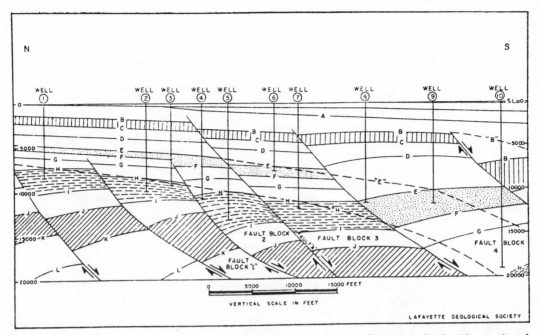

FIG. 11.29 Schematic and idealized cross section to illustrate deep north dip associated with a series of regional growth faults. Below 10,000–12,000 ft, structural north dip prevails. Figure also illustrates how cross sections A-A', B-B', and C-C' (Figs. 5–7) and regional structural maps (Figs. 16–21) were constructed. If a regional stratigraphic cross section were drawn on the basis of control provided by wells 1, 2, 5, 6, 7, 9, and 10, it would show south dip on horizons E and H, and southward thickening of interval E-H. Dashed lines that connect E and H correlation points in wells listed above show why this is true. If regional structural maps were constructed on either of the two dashed horizons, E or H, only regional south dip would appear. However, if all available well control were utilized, north dip would be present on E horizon in fault bock 4. All faults shown in this figure, except fault "A," are major growth faults. Fault "A" is a non-growth fault and there is no significant stratigraphic thickening between fault blocks 2 and 3.

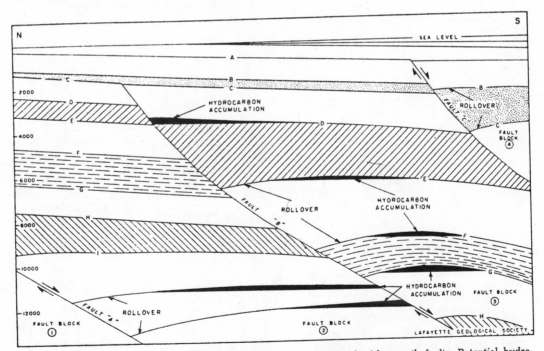

FIG. 11.30 Schematic cross section to illustrate phenomena associated with growth faults. Potential hydrocarbon traps are shown. Note (1) regional south dip of shallower beds; (2) north dip in fault block 2 below 10,000 ft; (3) thickening of interval C-F across fault "B"; (4) interval F-G is same thickness in fault blocks 2 and 3, showing that no growth took place on fault "B" during F-G time; (5) fault "B" had at least two periods of growth, one in pre-G time, and the other in C-F time; (6) rollover which increases with depth into faults "A," "B," and "C"; and (7) growth on fault "C" affects beds younger than those affected by fault "B." This is typical of Gulf Coast growth faults; *i.e.*, toward the Gulf of Mexico, age of growth faulting generally becomes younger.

After Meyerhoff, et al., 1968

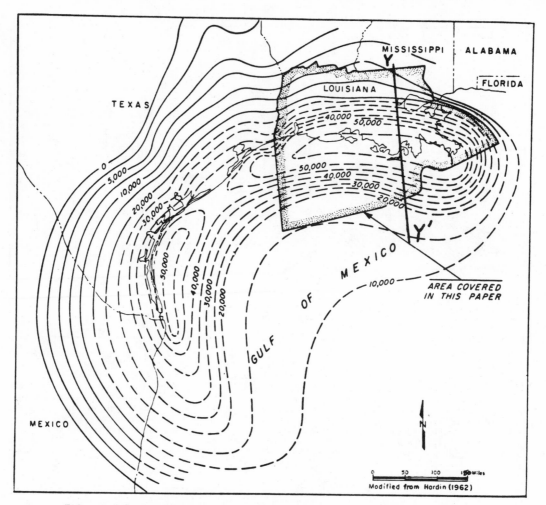

FIG. 11.31 Generalized isopachous map of the Cenozoic strata of Gulf Coast geosyncline.

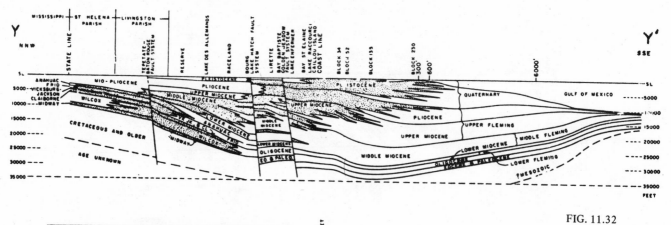

FIG. 11.32

NERITIC SHELF FACIES

After Meyerhoff, et al., 1968

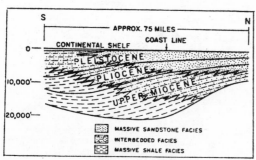

FIG. 11.33 Diagrammatic cross section of South Louisiana, showing gross lithologic facies of Gulf Coast geosyncline.

After Frey and Grimes, 1970

90

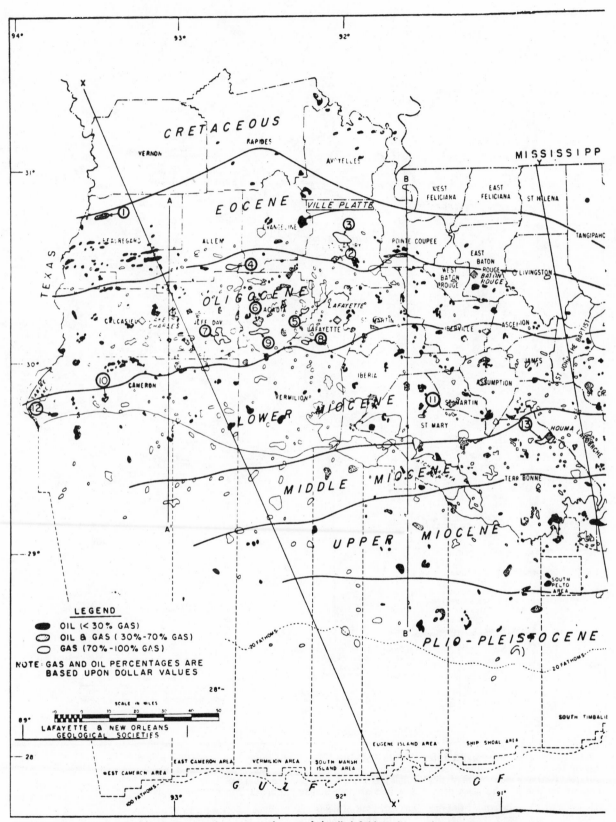

FIG. 11.34 Index to major producing trends, cross sections, and detailed field studies, south Louisiana. Lines
X-X', *Y-Y'*, *A-A'*, *B-B'* and *C-C'* are traces of cross sections of Figures 4–7. Subdivision of fields into categories
of gas, oil-gas, and oil fields is based on dollar value of gas and oil. Ratio used for computing dollar value is
15,000 cu ft of gas to 1 bbl of oil.   After Meyerhoff, et al., 1968

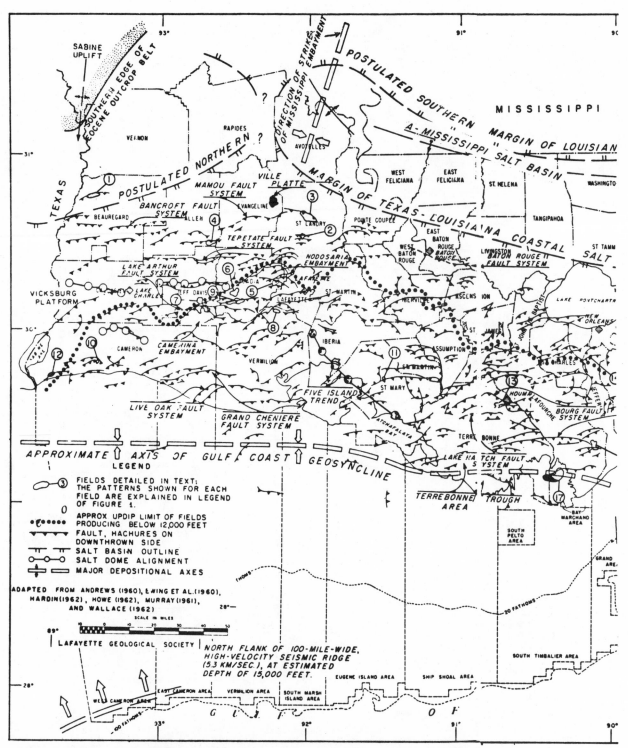

FIG. 11.35 Major structural features of south Louisiana. Most faults shown are regional or major growth faults. Other structural features, including some that may be basement controlled, are illustrated. Northern limit of most south Louisiana fields which produce from sands below 12,000 ft is shown by line of solid black dots. The writers are indebted to Gordon I. Atwater for supplying data with which to determine this line. Northern limit of fields that produce below a depth of 12,000 ft coincides very closely with that of the northernmost major Frio growth faults. Scarcity of faults offshore reflects lack of published information from this area.

After Meyerhoff, et al., 1968

92

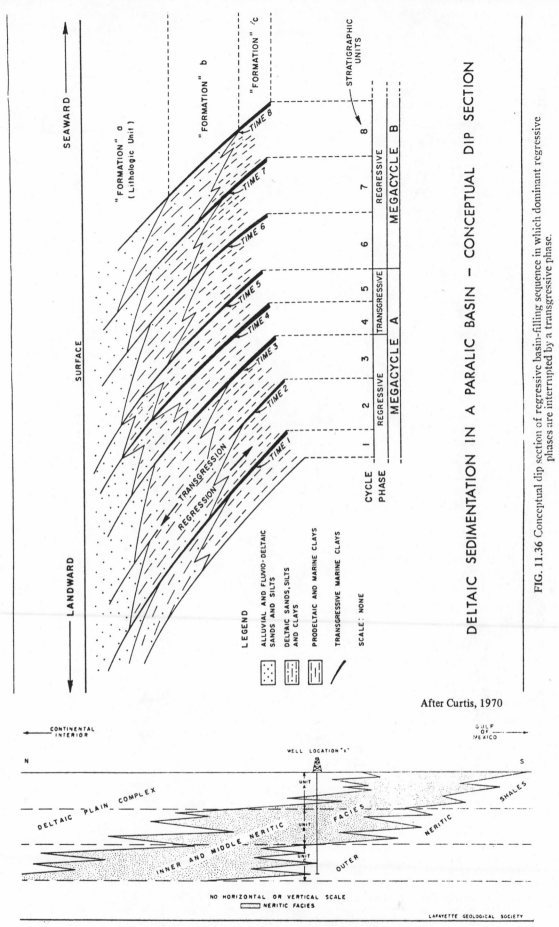

LEGEND

	ALLUVIAL AND FLUVIO-DELTAIC SANDS AND SILTS
	DELTAIC SANDS, SILTS AND CLAYS
	PRODELTAIC AND MARINE CLAYS
	TRANSGRESSIVE MARINE CLAYS

SCALE: NONE

DELTAIC SEDIMENTATION IN A PARALIC BASIN — CONCEPTUAL DIP SECTION

FIG. 11.36 Conceptual dip section of regressive basin-filling sequence in which dominant regressive phases are interrupted by a transgressive phase.

After Curtis, 1970

FIG. 11.37 Schematic and idealized diagram showing vertical and lateral relationships between three principal depositional environments in Gulf Coast geosyncline.

After Meyerhoff, et al., 1968

93

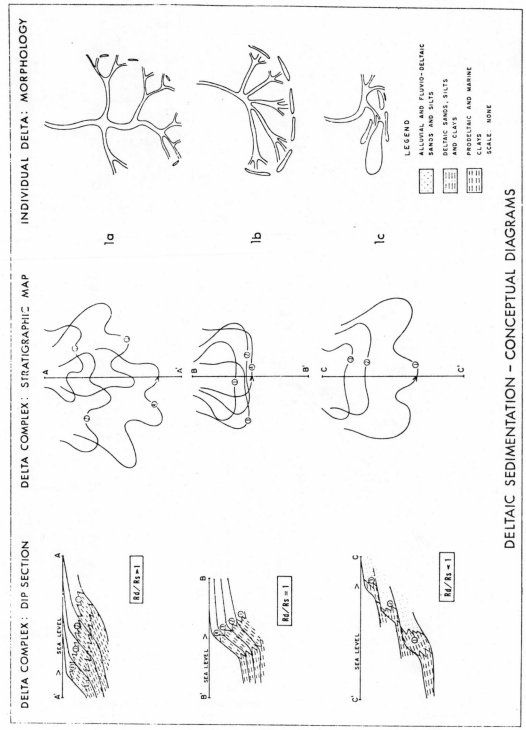

DELTA COMPLEX: DIP SECTION   DELTA COMPLEX: STRATIGRAPHIC MAP   INDIVIDUAL DELTA: MORPHOLOGY

$Rd/Rs > 1$

$Rd/Rs = 1$

$Rd/Rs < 1$

1a

1b

1c

LEGEND

ALLUVIAL AND FLUVIO-DELTAIC
SANDS AND SILTS

DELTAIC SANDS, SILTS
AND CLAYS

PRODELTAIC AND MARINE
CLAYS

SCALE: NONE

DELTAIC SEDIMENTATION – CONCEPTUAL DIAGRAMS

FIG. 11.38 Conceptual diagrams of variations in delta characteristics resulting from variations in ratio between rate of deposition and rate of subsidence (Rd/Rs).

After Curtis, 1970

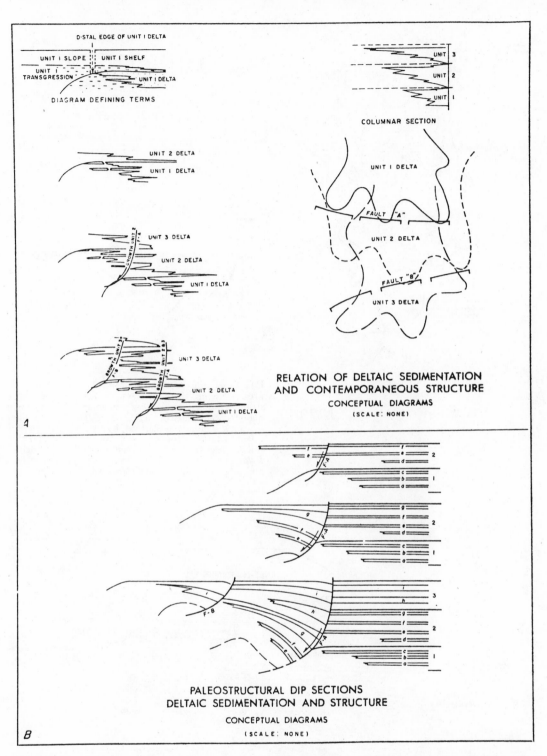

FIG. 11.39 Conceptual diagrams showing initiation of slump faulting as a delta progrades beyond distal end of an older delta. *A*, Fault A develops at distal end of unit 1 as unit 2 progrades beyond distal end of unit 1; fault B develops at distal end of unit 2 as unit 3 progrades beyond distal end of unit 2. Fault A movement is contemporaneous with unit 2 and later sedimentation; fault B movement is contemporaneous with unit 3 and later sedimentation. *B*, Successive stages in development of counterregional dip and shale uplift during syndepositional faulting.

After Curtis, 1970

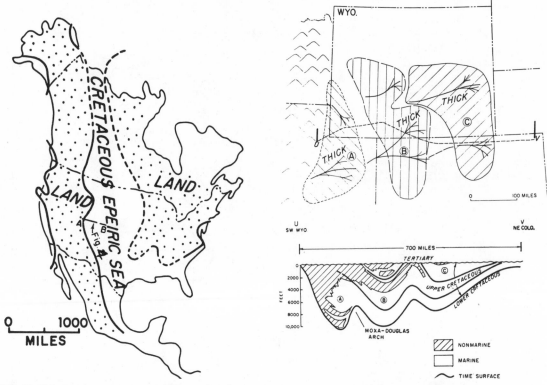

FIG. 11.40 Index map showing geographic distribution of Cretaceous seaway (after Gill and Cobban, 1966).

FIG. 11.41 *Above,* Map of central Rocky Mountain area showing thick wedges of Upper Cretaceous strata; A, older than early Campanian; B, Campanian and early Maestrichtian; C, Maestrichtian; wedges of thick strata are formed by two deltaic centers (depocenters) prograding eastward; lines within thick areas represent probable position of deltas. *Below,* cross section UV showing vertical dimensions and migration in time and space of depocenters; position of boundary between B and C is complicated by uplift and truncation before deposition of Tertiary rocks.

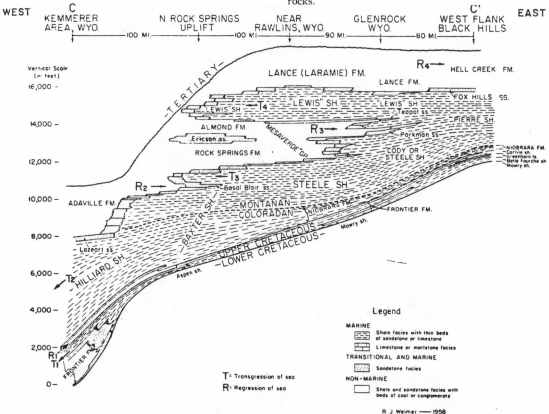

FIG. 11.42 Diagrammatic restored section of Upper Cretaceous rocks extending from southwest Wyoming to west flank of Black Hills in northeast Wyoming. Tertiary rocks regionally cover erosional surface of Cretaceous strata. Diagram structurally distorts this surface.

After Weimer, 1960

96

DELTAIC AND ASSOCIATED ENVIRONMENTS

Books or Special Publications

Amer. Assoc. Petrol. Geol. Bull., no. 8, August, 1971, (special issue on deltas and petroleum): v. 55.

Bernard, H. A., Major, C. F., Parrott, B. S., and LeBlanc, R. J., Sr., 1970, Recent sediments of southeast Texas: Texas Bur. Econ. Geol. Guidebook no. 11, Austin, Texas.

Dikkers, A. J. (ed.), Deltaic deposits and petroleum: Proceedings Panel 4, 9th World Petroleum Congress, Tokyo, May 11-16, 1975 (in press).

*Fisher, W.L.,et al (eds.) 1969, Delta Systems in the Exploration for Oil and Gas - A Research Colloquim, Bur. of Econ. Geol., The Univ. of Texas, Austin, Texas, 78 p. 110 illustrations, 24 p. selected references.

Geological Society of America, Carboniferous of the Southeastern United States, Sp. Paper 148.

Meyerhoff, A. A. (ed.), 1968, Geology of Natural Gas in south Louisiana: in Beebe, B. W. and Curtis, B. (eds.), Natural Gases of North America, Amer. Assoc. Petrol. Geol. Memoir 9, p. 376-581.

*Morgan, J. P., (ed.), 1970, Deltaic sedimentation, modern and ancient: Soc. Econ. Paleo. Min. Sp. Pub. no. 15, 312 p.

Shirley, M. A., (ed.), 1966, Deltas in their geologic framework, Houston Geol. Soc., Houston, Texas, 251 p.

DELTAIC ENVIRONMENTS - QUATERNARY

*Allen, J. R. L., 1965, Late Quaternary Niger delta, and adjacent areas: sedimentary environments and lithofacies: Amer. Assoc. Petrol. Geol. Bull., v. 49, p. 547-600.

Bates, C. C., 1953, Rational theory of delta formation: Amer. Assoc. Petrol. Geol. Bull., v. 37, p. 2119-2162.

Born, S. M., 1972, Late Quaternary history deltaic sedimentation and mudlump formation at Pyramid Lake, Nevada: Desert Research Inst., Univ. of Nevada Sp. Pub., 97 p.

Coleman, J. M., 1966, Ecological changes in a massive fresh-water clay sequence: Trans. Gulf. Coast. Assoc. Geol. Soc., v. 15, p. 159-174.

_____, 1969, Brahmaputra River: channel processes and sedimentation: Sedimentary Geology, v. 3, p. 131-237.

Coleman, J. M. and Gagliano, S. M., 1964, Cyclic sedimentation in the Mississippi River deltaic plain: Gulf Coast Assoc. Geol. Soc. Trans., v. 14, p. 67-80.

Coleman, J. M. and Gagliano, S. M., 1965, Sedimentary structures: Mississippi River deltaic plain: Soc. Econ. Paleo. and Min., Sp. Pub. no. 12, p. 133-148.

Coleman, J. M., Gagliano, S. M. and Smith, W. G., 1970, Sedimentation in a Malaysian high tide tropical delta: Soc. Econ. Paleo. Min. Sp. Pub. 15, p. 185-197.

Coleman, J. M., Gagliano, S. M. and Webb, J. E., 1964, Minor sedimentary structures in a prograding distributary: Marine Geol., v. 1, p. 240-258.

Dunbar, C. O. and Rodgers, J., 1957, Principles of stratigraphy, John Wiley and Sons.

Fisk, H. N., 1961, Barfinger sands of the Mississippi delta: in Osmond, J. C. and Peterson, J. A., (eds.) Geometry of Sandstone Bodies, Amer. Assoc. Petrol. Geol., p. 29-52.

Fisk, H. N., et al., 1954, Sedimentary framework of the modern Mississippi delta: Jour. Sed. Petrology, v. 24, p. 76-99.

Frazier, D. E., 1967, Recent deltaic deposits of the Mississippi River, their development and chronology: Gulf Coast Assoc. Geol. Socs. Trans., v. 17, p. 287-315.

Gagliano, S. M. and McIntire, W. G., 1968, Delta components in Recent and ancient deltaic sedimentation: A comparison: Louisiana State Univ. Coastal Studies Inst.

Galloway, W. E. and Brown, L. F., Jr., 1972, Depositional systems and shelf-slope relationships in upper Pennsylvanian rocks, north central Texas, Texas Bur. of Econ. Geol. Rep. Inv. 75, 62 p.

*Gould, H. R., 1970, The Mississippi delta complex: Soc. Econ. Paleo. and Min., Sp. Pub. 15, p. 3-30.

Ho, C. and Coleman, J. M., 1969, Consolidation and cementation of Recent sediments in the Atchafalaya Basin: Geol. Soc. Amer. Bull., v. 80, no. 2, p. 183-191.

Kholief, M. M., Hilmy, E., and Shahat, A., 1969, Geological and mineralogical studies of some sand deposits in the Nile Delta, U. A. R.: Jour. Sedimentary Petrology, v. 39, p. 1520-1530.

Kolb, C. R. and Van Lopik, J. R., 1966, Depositional environments of the Mississippi River deltaic plain - Southeastern Louisiana: in Shirley, M. A. (ed.), Deltas in their Geologic Framework, Houston Geol. Soc., p. 17-61.

LeBlanc, R. J., 1972, Geometry of sandstone reservoirs: Amer. Assoc. Petrol. Geol. Memoir 18, p. 133-177, (also in AAPG Reprint series no. 7).

MacKay, J. R., 1963, The MacKenzie Delta area, N. W. T.: Ottowa, Canada Geol. Survey, Geog. Branch, Memoir 8, 202 p.

Mathews, W. H. and Shepard, F. P., 1962, Sedimentation of Fraser River delta, British Columbia: Amer. Assoc. Petrol. Geol. Bull., v. 46, no. 8, p. 1416-1443.

Meckel. L. D., 1972, Anatomy of distributary channel - fill deposits in Recent mud deltas (abs.): Amer. Assoc. Petrol. Geol. Bull., v. 56, p. 639.

Moore, G. T., and Asquith, D. O., 1971, Delta: Term and Concept: Bull. Geol. Soc. Amer., v. 82, p. 2563-2568.

*Morgan, J. P., 1970a, Deltas--A resume: Jour. Geol. Educ., v. 18, no. 3, p. 107-117.

_____, 1970b, Depositional processes and products in the deltaic environment: Soc. Econ. Paleo. and Min. Sp. Pub. 15, p. 31-47.

Morgan, J. P., Coleman, J. M. and Gagliano, S. M., 1968, Mudlumps: diapiric structures in Mississippi delta sediments: in Diapirism and diapirs,Memoir no. 8, Amer. Assoc, Petrol. Geol., Tulsa, Okla., p. 145-161.

*Oomkens, E., 1974, Lithofacies relations in the Late Quaternary Niger delta complex., Sedimentology, v. 21, p. 195-222.

Scruton, P. C., 1960, Delta building and the deltaic sequence: in Recent Sediments, Northwest Gulf of Mexico, 1951-1958, Amer. Assoc. of Petrol. Geol., Tulsa, Okla., p. 82-102.

Shepard, F. P., 1956, Marginal sediments of the Mississippi delta: Amer. Assoc. Petrol. Geol. Bull., v. 40, p. 2537-2623.

_____, 1960, Mississippi delta: marginal environments, sediments and growth: in Shepard, et al. (eds.), Recent Sediments, Northwest Gulf of Mexico: Amer. Assoc. Petrol. Geol., Tulsa, Okla.

_____, 1973, Sea floor off Magdalena Delta and Santa Marta area, Colombia: Geol. Soc. Amer. Bull., v. 84, p. 1955-1972.

Short, K. C. and Stauble, A. J., 1967, Outline of geology of Niger delta: Amer. Assoc. Petrol. Geol. Bull., v. 51, p. 761-779.

Van Andel, T. J., 1967, The Orinoco Delta: Jour. Sed. Petrol., v. 37, p. 297-310.

Wright, L. D. and Coleman, J. M., 1973, Variations in morphology of major river deltas as functions of ocean wave and river discharge regimes: Amer. Assoc. Petrol. Geol. Bull., v. 57, no. 2, p. 370-398.

Asquith, D. O., 1970, Depositional topography and major marine environments, Late Cretaceous, Wyoming: Amer. Assoc. Petrol Geol. Bull., v. 54, no. 7, p. 1184-1224.

Bruce, C. F. and Parker, E. R., 1975, Structural features and hydrocarbon deposits in the MacKenzie Delta: 9th World Petroleum Congress Proc., Panel 4, Tokyo.

Carrigy, M. A., 1966, Lithology of the Athabaska Oil Sands: Res. Council of Alberta Bull. 18, p. 1-29.

Curtis, D. M., 1970, Miocene deltaic sedimentation, Louisiana Gulf Coast: Soc. Econ. Paleo. and Min. Sp. Pub. 15, p. 293-308.

Davis, T. L., 1974, Seismic investigation of Late Cretaceous faulting along east flank of the central Front Range, Colorado: PhD Thesis T-1681, Colorado School of Mines, (unpub.).

Ecker, G. D., Jr., 1971, Peoria Field, Arapahoe County, Colorado: The Mountain Geologist, v. 8, no. 3, p. 141-150.

Ferm, J. C., 1974, Carboniferous environmental models in eastern United States and their significance: Geol. Soc. Amer. Sp. Paper 148, p. 79-95; Selected Bibliography, p. 337-355.

Ferm, J. C. and Williams, E. G., 1963, Model for cyclic sedimentation in the Appalachian Pennsylvanian (abs.): Amer. Assoc. Petrol. Geol. Bull., v. 47, no. 2, p. 356.

Fisher, W. L. and McGowan, J. H., 1969, Depositional systems in the Wilcox Group (Eocene) of Texas and their relationship to the occurrence of oil and gas: Amer. Assoc. Petrol. Geol. Bull., v. 53, p. 30-54.

Frey, M. G. and Grimes, W. H., 1970, Bay Marchand--Timbalier--Caillou Island Salt Complex, Louisiana: in Halbouty, M. T. (ed.), Geology of Giant Petroleum Fields, Amer. Assoc. Petrol. Geol. Memoir 14, p. 277-291.

Gill, J. R., 1973, Stratigraphy and geologic history of the Montana group and equivalent rocks, Montana, Wyoming and North and South Dakota: U. S. Geol. Survey Prof. Paper 776, 37 p.

Gill, J. R. and Cobban, W. A., 1966, The Red Bird section of the Upper Cretaceous Pierre Shale in Wyoming: U. S. Geol. Survey Prof. Paper 393-A, 73 p.

Gill, J. R., Cobban, W. A. and Schultz, L. G., 1972, Stratigraphy and composition of the Sharon Springs, Member of the Pierre Shale in Western Kansas: U. S. Geol. Survey Prof. Paper 728, 50 p.

Hubert, J., et al., 1972, Sedimentology of Upper Cretaceous Cody-Parkman delta, southwestern Powder River Basin, Wyoming: Geol. Soc. Amer. Bull., v. 83, p. 1649-1670

MacMillan, L. T., 1974, Stratigraphy of the South Platte Formation (Lower Cretaceous), Morrison--Weaver Gulch area, Jefferson County, Colorado: Colorado School of Mines, MSc Thesis T-1626, (unpub.), 86 p.

Magnier, Ph., Oki, T. and Kartaadiputra, L. W., 1975, The Mahakam Delta, Kalimantan, Indonesia: 9th World Petroleum Congress Proc., Panel 4, Tokyo.

McBride, E. F., 1974, Significance of color in red, green, purple, olive, brown and gray beds of Difunta group, Northeastern Mexico: Jour. Sed. Petrology, v. 44, no. 3, p. 760-773.

*McGregor, A. A., and Biggs, C. A., 1968, Bell Creek Field, Montana: a rich stratigraphic trap: Amer. Assoc. Petrol. Geol. Bull., v. 52, no. 10, p. 1869-1887.

Ovanesov,G.P., et al.,1975, Palaeodeltaic sediments and methods of petroleum exploration in the U. S. S. R.: 9th World Petroleum Congress Proc., Panel 4, Tokyo.

Rainwater, E. H., 1966, Geologic significance of deltas: in Shirley, M. L., (ed.), Deltas in their Geologic Framework, Houston Geol. Soc., Houston, Texas, p. 1-15.

Thompson, G. G., 1972, Palynologic correlation and environmental analysis within the marine Mancos Shale of southwestern Colorado, Jour. Sed. Petrology, v. 42, no. 2, p. 287.

Van de Graaff, F. R., 1972, Fluvial-deltaic facies of the Castlegate Sandstone (Cretaceous), east central Utah, Jour. Sed. Petrology, v. 42, no. 3, p. 558.

Weber, K. J. and Daukoru, R., 1975, Petroleum Geology of the Niger Delta: 9th World Petroleum Congress Proc., Panel 4, Tokyo.

Weimer, R. J., 1960, Upper Cretaceous stratigraphy, Rocky Mountain area: Amer. Assoc. Petrol. Geol. Bull., v. 44, no. 1, p. 1-20.

_____, 1970, Late Cretaceous deltas, Rocky Mountain region: Soc. Econ. Paleo. and Min. Sp. Pub. 15, p. 270-292.

_____, 1971, Deltas and petroleum: Foreword: Amer. Assoc. Petrol. Geol., v. 55, no. 8. p. 1135-1136.

* _____, 1973, A guide to uppermost Cretaceous stratigraphy, central Front Range, Colorado: deltaic sedimentation, growth faulting and early Laramide crustal movement: The Mountain Geologist, v. 10, no. 3, p. 53-97.

Weimer, R. J. and Land, C. B., 1972, Field guide to Dakota Group (Cretaceous) stratigraphy, Golden-Morrison area, Colorado: The Mountain Geologist, v. 9, no. 2-3, p. 241-267.

Weimer, R. J. and Land, C. B., 1975, Maestrichtian deltaic and interdeltaic sedimentation, Rocky Mountain Region: in Special volume on Cretaceous deposits, Geol. Assoc. Canada, Sp. Paper (in press).

Weimer, R. J., Land, C. B. and MacMillan, L. T., 1974, A stratigraphic model for distributary channels, (J) and muddy sandstones, Rocky Mountain Region (abs.): Amer. Assoc. Petrol. Geol. Ann. Meetings Abstracts, v. 1, p. 97.

OUTLINE FOR LECTURE 9
(12)

BARRIER ISLAND (SHORELINE) AND ASSOCIATED ENVIRONMENTS

1. Components and terminology of barrier island systems (Figs. 12.1-12.4)

   a) Beach (back shore, fore shore), shore face, dunes, beach ridge, swale, barrier flat (wash-overs), tidal inlet (or estuary).

   b) Terminology problems

   offshore bar versus barrier bar

   shoreline for reference

   ocean versus lagoon

   c) Shorelines of emergence and submergence

2. Processes controlling development, modification and lateral changes of shoreline sands (includes shore face).

   a) Wave-generated currents in shore face zone (effective wave base).

   b) Tide-and wave-generated currents - beach, inlets, tidal channels.

   c) Storm effects superimposed on normal processes.

   d) Longshore drift - movement of sand along littoral zone from source areas which may be: a)rivers, b) cannibalizing along shoreline, c) reworking of ancient deposit on sea floor during submergence.

   e) Eolian - coastal dunes (processes described in Lecture 10)

   f) Ground water table fluctuations in ridge and swale topography; oxidation processes; root systems.

   g) Biogenic: response of organisms making biogenic structures to energy, rates of sedimentation and food supply.

   h) Highest rates of sedimentation in general shoreline zone; slower rates landward and seaward; rates of lateral accretion high compared to vertical accumulation; high energy deposits prograde over those of lower energy, therefore coarsening upward sequence (Fig. 12.5) (except in tidal channel area where reverse is found).

   i) Barrier island (shoreline) accretes seaward by addition of sand in beach zone (forming beach ridge or chenier) and also in direction of long shore drift.

3. Genetic Units (facies-lithologic associations)

   a) Barrier island - lagoon sequence - (Fig. 12.5,12.30-12.32). Example - Galveston Island, Central Texas Coast. See vertical sections showing variations in structures and textures (Fig. 12.5).

103

Tidal channel-tidal delta sequence that forms where tidal inlet cuts barrier island.

Chenier plain - where shoreline progrades by alternating additions of sand and mud to beach area.

b) Barrier island - tidal channel (estuary or sound) - tidal flat - salt marsh sequences (Figs. 12.6-12.8). Example: Central Georgia Coast, Sapelo Island area, North Sea-Holland and Germany.

Vertical sections similar to (a) above except with greater occurrence of tidal channels (see Fig. 13.26, after Land).

c) Additional examples of facies associations in shoreline deposits are presented in Lecture 13 - Deltaic versus Interdeltaic environments.

d) Characteristics of barrier island sand bodies (Table 8.4).

4. Tectonics and sedimentation

a) Rates of deposition (Rd) compared with rates of subsidence (Rs) controls thickness of shoreline deposits.

1) Rd/Rs > 1 = Progradation (regression) with long linear multilateral sand bodies 20 to 40 feet thick; stable tectonic setting. Thickness of sand body controlled by effective wave base; the length by geomorphology of shoreline; width by sand supply, water depth on shelf and duration of prograding process.

2) Rd/Rs = 1 = multistory sand bodies; many linear genetic units stacked vertically because of basin-wide subsidence or localized growth faulting.

3) Rd/Rs < 1 = Widely spaced isolated narrow linear bars 20 to 30 feet resting on coastal plain deposits. Sand bars do not show vertical segregation of lithologies like regressive deposit (1 above).

5. Importance of barrier island(shoreline) sequences in petroleum exploration.

a) Important stratigraphic traps because long linear porous and permeable bar sands may be enclosed by impermeable shales and siltstone; high predictability of facies trends.

b) Shoreline sands that are buried rapidly and onlapped by marine shales seem to be most favorable for petroleum (temporary still stands of shoreline on overall transgressive cycle).

c) Shoreline sands on overall progradation cycle may not develop early up-dip seals of porosity and permeability thus loosing early formed gases to atmosphere; after greater depth of burial traps may not be close enough to source beds for migration and accumulation.

104

6. Importance of barrier island (shoreline) sequences in coal and unanium exploration.
   a) Coals are commonly found in coastal plain sequences marginal to and inland from barrier islands. Recognition of barrier bars in record may serve as guide to area of coal deposition (environment = marsh or coastal swamp); minor lenticular coal may form as swale deposit; abandoned barrier islands on regressive cycle (falling sea level) may form topographic ridges which control drainage and coal swamps may develop in former lagoonal area. Example: Okefenochee Swamp, Southern Georgia.
   b) Barrier bars generally have excellent porosity and permeability in upper portion; therefore a good host rock for uranium. However, sands usually have low detrital carbonaceous content because of oxidation or digestion by organisms. Generally, not a favorable setting for uranium occurrences.
7. Examples of ancient petroleum - producing sequences.
   a) Upper Cretaceous, Patrick Draw Field, Wyoming (75,000,000 bbls), Figs. 12.9-12.23.
   b) Lower Cretaceous, Bell Creek Field, Montana, (150,000,000 bbls., second largest field in Montana), Figs. 12.23-12.32.
8. Examples of barrier bar- beach sandstones available for study during seminar: Outcrop - Fox Hills Sandstone (Upper Cretaceous, White Rocks); Cores - Almond Formation, Patrick Draw Field, Upper Cretaceous, Wyoming); Parkman Sandstone, Manning Field (Upper Cretaceous, Wyoming); Muddy Sandstone, Bell Creek Field (Lower Cretaceous, Montana).

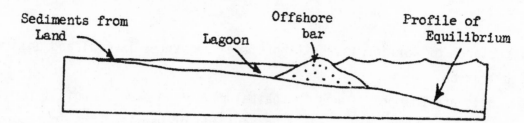

FIG. 12.1 Cross section showing the features of the shore zone of a low-lying coast.

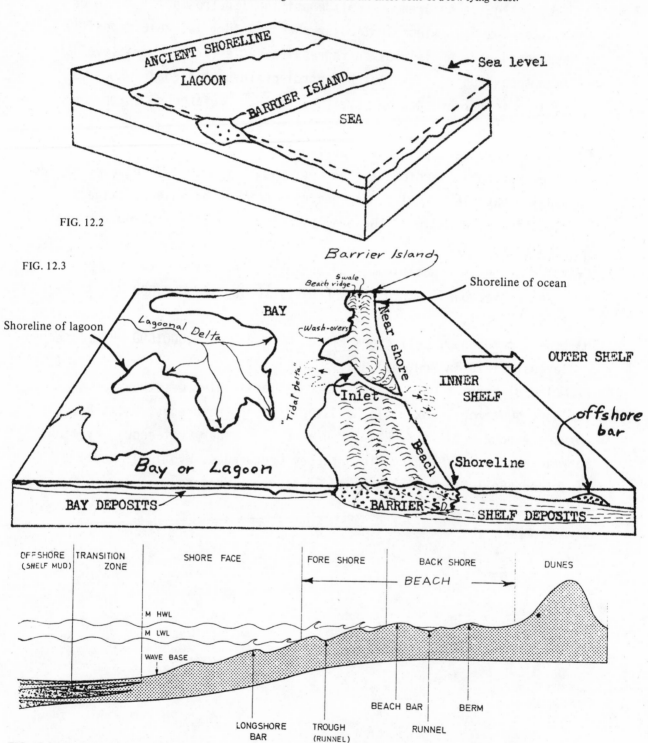

FIG. 12.2

FIG. 12.3

FIG. 12.4 Schematic representation of the terminology of the various geomorphic units of a beach profile. Various geomorphic features of a beach as well as transition to shelf mud are shown. The terminology is mainly based on EMERY (1960a)

106　　　　　　After Reineck and Singh, 1973

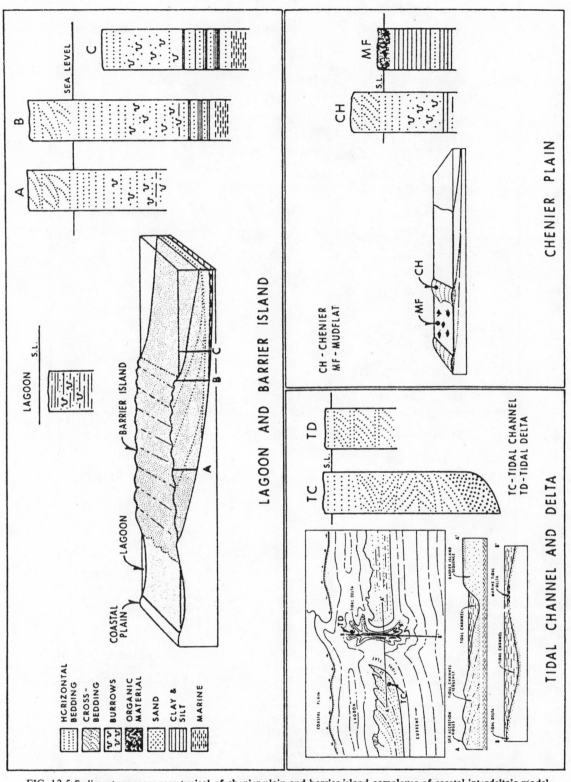

FIG. 12.5 Sedimentary sequences typical of chenier-plain and barrier-island complexes of coastal-interdeltaic model of clastic sedimentation.

After LeBlanc, 1972

107

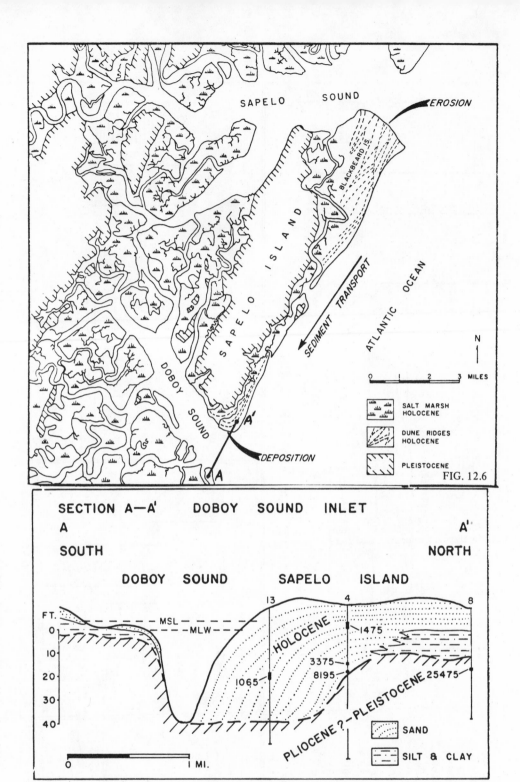

FIG. 12.6

SECTION A—A'   DOBOY   SOUND   INLET

A   A'

SOUTH   NORTH

DOBOY   SOUND   SAPELO   ISLAND

HOLOCENE

PLIOCENE ? – PLEISTOCENE

SAND

SILT & CLAY

FIG. 12.7 Cross section at Doboy Sound inlet, Georgia; vertical exaggeration 100 to 1. *See* Figure
for location and Figure for explanation of symbols.

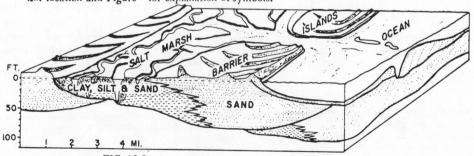

FIG. 12.8 Idealized diagram of a migrating barrier island

108

After Hoyt and Henry, 1967

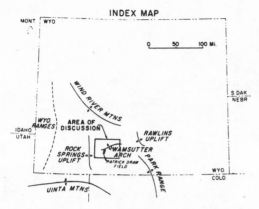

FIG. 12.9 Index map showing location of Patrick Draw field and area of discussion in relation to other tectonic elements in southwest Wyoming.

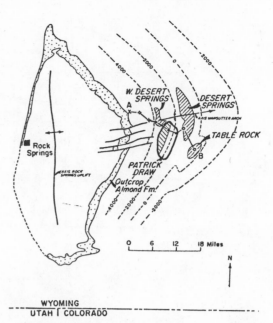

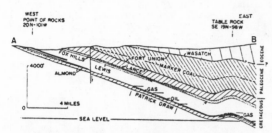

FIG. 12.11 West-east structural cross section A-B from surface section of Almond Formation to Table Rock field. Stratigraphic changes and position of Patrick Draw field are indicated. Section is from just west of locality A to locality B, Figures 2 and 5.

FIG. 12.10 Regional structural contour map showing principal petroleum fields producing from Almond Formation on Wamsutter arch. Locations of structural cross section (Fig. 3) and electric-log correlation section A-B (Fig. 4) are indicated. Dashed lines are structural contours in feet; structural datum is top of Almond Formation. Surface elevations in area range from 6,500 to 7,500 ft. Stippled area is outcrop of Almond Formation on flanks of Rock Springs uplift. Diagonal ruling is gas-productive area. Unruled area in Patrick Draw field is oil-productive.

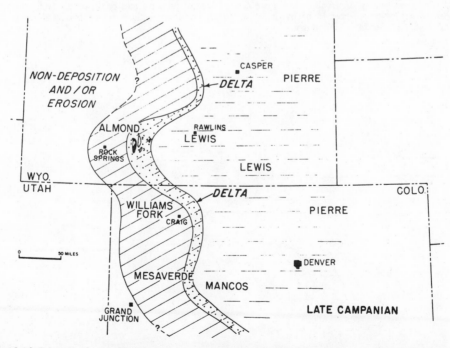

FIG. 12.12 Generalized regional lithofacies map showing correlation of upper part of Almond in Wamsutter arch fields and adjacent areas. Environmental interpretation: horizontal ruling = neritic shale and siltstone; diagonal ruling = coastal-plain deposits of impermeable coal-bearing claystone, siltstone, sandstone; mixed stippling and diagonal ruling = zone of intertonguing porous and permeable barrier-bar sandstone beds (shoreline) and coastal-plain deposits (as above). Petroleum fields: 1 = Patrick Draw and West Desert Springs; 2 = Desert Springs; 3 = Table Rock; 4 = Wamsutter.

After Weimer, 1966

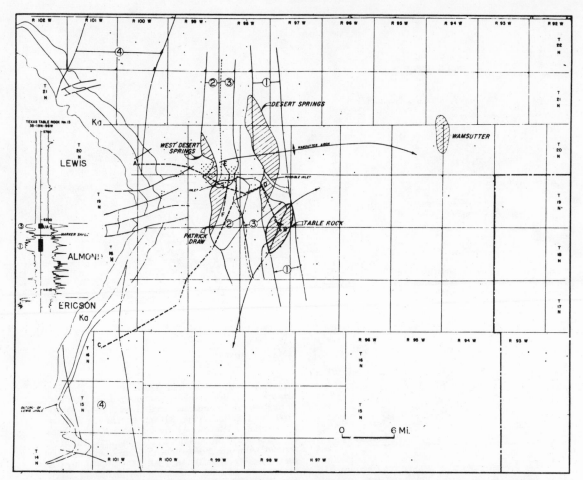

FIG. 12.13 Map showing areal distribution of four porous and permeable sandstone zones in upper 100 ft. of Almond Formation. Stratigraphic positions of bar-sandstone bodies 1, 2, 3, and 4 are shown on Figure 11. (Patrick Draw producing sandstone beds referred to in field as UA-5.) Distribution of porosity and permeability in producing interval at Table Rock and Desert Springs and in surface exposures also is shown. Ka = outcrop of Almond Formation; hachures indicate gas-producing areas in each belt of porous sandstone. Impermeable sandstone beds of Intervals 1 and 4 are east of belt of porosity and permeability (refer to Figs. 4, 11). Sandstone bodies are inferred to be barrier-bars. Control wells are solid dots; field wells are not shown. Location of Figure 11 (section C-D) shown.

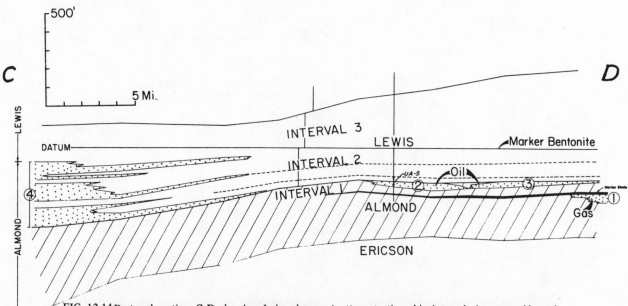

FIG. 12.14 Restored section C-D showing facies changes in time-stratigraphic intervals in upper Almond Formation and Lewis Shale. Stratigraphic position of inferred barrier-bar sandstone bodies 1, 2, 3, and 4 in upper Almond also shown. Line of section indicated on Figures 12, 14, and 15. Section from electric logs of indicated wells. Diagonal ruling—non-marine sediments; stippled pattern—marine and transitional sandstone with some siltstone and shale; unmarked area in middle of diagram—marine shale.

After Weimer, 1966

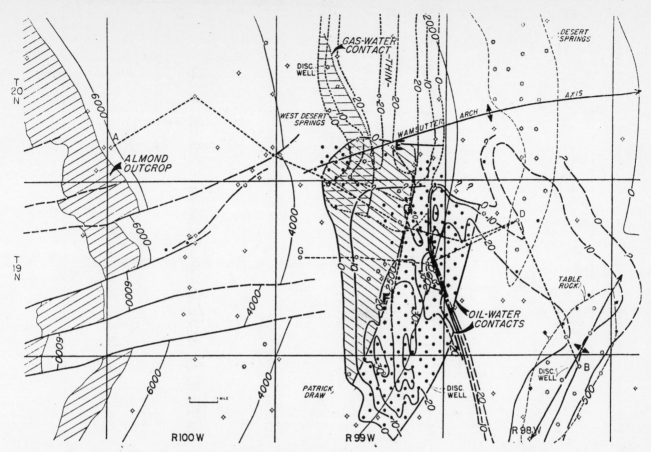

FIG. 12.15 Isopachous map of uppermost Almond sandstone bodies (UA-5) in Patrick Draw (solid lines), Table Rock (long dashes), and West Desert Springs (short dashes) area. Isopachous contours are superimposed on structural contour map whose structural datum is top of Almond Formation. Isopachous interval is 10 ft.; structural contour interval is 2,000 ft. unless otherwise noted.

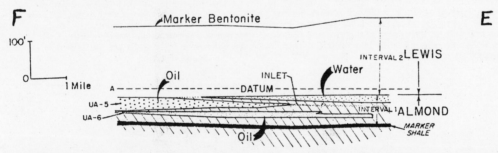

FIG. 12.16 South-north restored section F-E prepared from cores and electric logs showing northern pinch-out of main Patrick Draw producing sandstone (UA-5). Stratigraphic position of UA-6 producing sandstone also indicated. Note southward thickening of UA-5 and contact of UA-5 and UA-6 sandstone beds in sec. 23. Area where sandstone beds are in contact is shown on Figure 5. Location of section is shown on Figures 5 and 6.

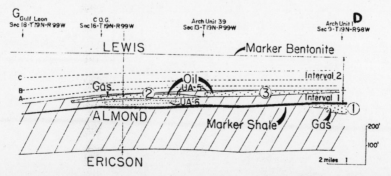

After Weimer, 1966

FIG. 12.17 West-east restored secton G-D across Patrick Draw field showing stratigraphic position of pr' ductive sandstones. Bar 1—main gas-productive sandstone zone, Desert Springs and Table Rock fields. Bars and 3 (UA-5)—oil and gas-productive at Patrick Draw field. Time-stratigraphic Intervals 1 and 2 discuss in text are indicated. Dashed lines labeled A, B, C in Lewis are marker beds. Line of section shown on Fi ures 5 and 6.

111

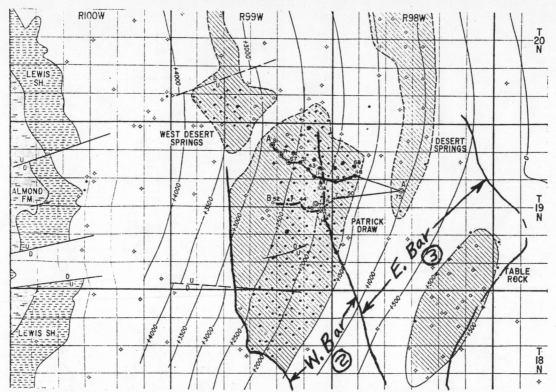

FIG. 12.18 Structure contour map on top of Almond Formation. Circled well symbols show location of cores used in this study. Numbers identify wells referred to in figures or text. (Compiled from Lawson and Crowson, 1961; Mees, et al., 1961; and May, 1961.)

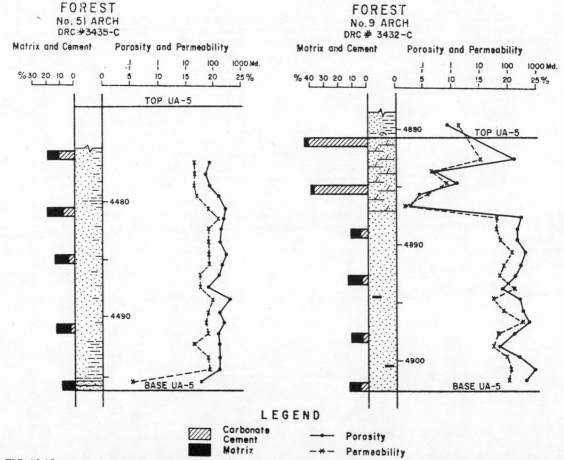

FIG. 12.19 Vertical variation of porosity and permeability of Patrick Draw UA-5 sandstone and relationship to variations in carbonate cement and matrix content. Abundance of matrix and carbonate cement, based on thin-section point counts, shown as percent of the total rock (including pore space).

After McCubbin and Brady, 1969

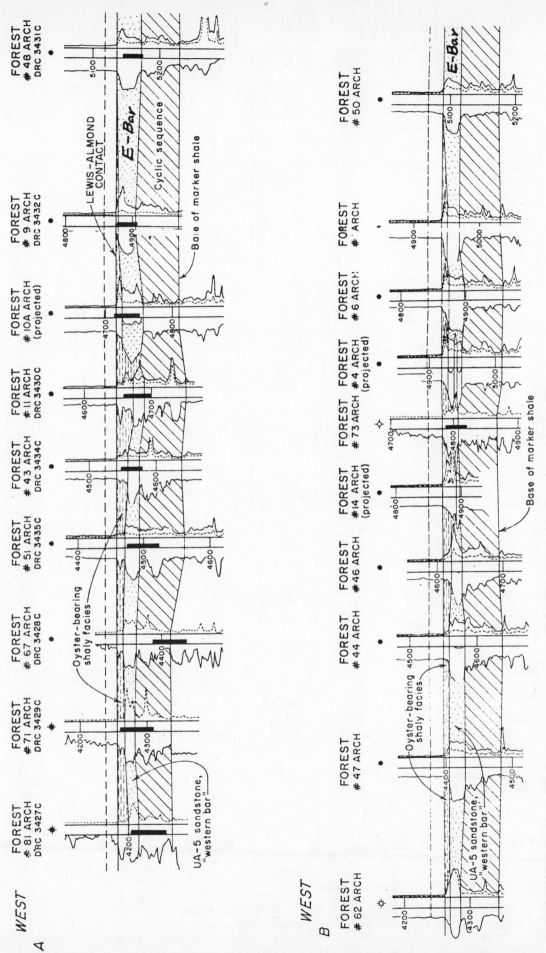

FIG. 12.20 Stratigraphic cross sections of upper Almond Formation, Patrick Draw area, showing major stratigraphic units. Correlations are based on electric logs and core control. Vertical bars show intervals of core control. Locations of sections shown on Figs. 3 and 4.

After McCubbin and Brady, 1969

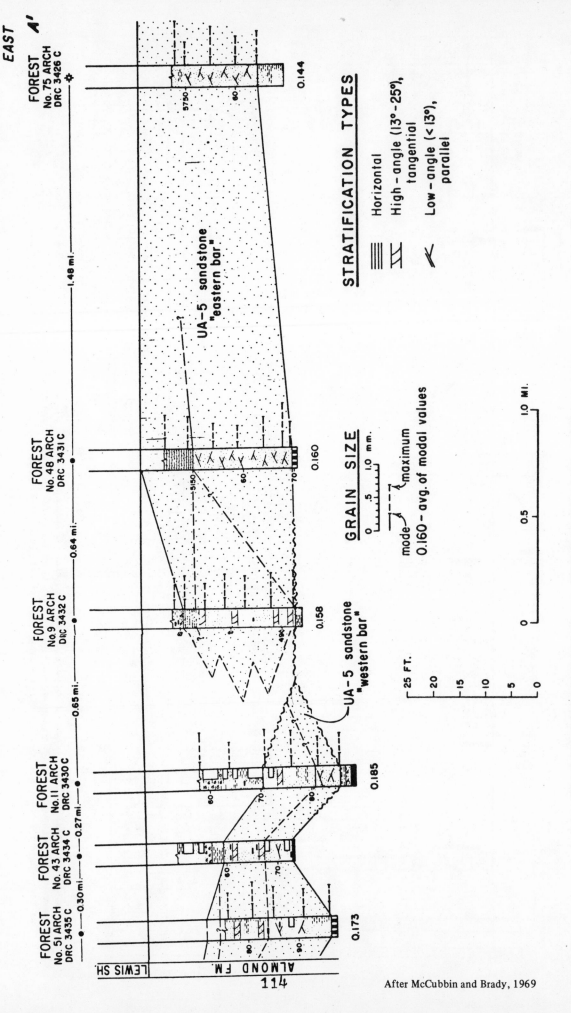

FIG. 12.21 Distribution of grain sizes and stratification types, Patrick Draw UA-5 sandstone, Patrick Draw area. Approximate boundaries of zones or facies characterized by different stratification types are shown by dashed lines.

STRATIFICATION TYPES

Horizontal

High-angle (13°-25°), tangential

Low-angle (<13°), parallel

GRAIN SIZE

0   .5   1.0 mm.

mode — maximum
0.160 — avg. of modal values

0   0.5   1.0 MI.

25 FT.
20
15
10
5
0

UA-5 sandstone "eastern bar"

UA-5 sandstone "western bar"

EAST A'

FOREST No. 75 ARCH DRC 3426 C
FOREST No. 48 ARCH DRC 3431 C
FOREST No. 9 ARCH DRC 3432 C
FOREST No. 11 ARCH DRC 3430 C
FOREST No. 43 ARCH DRC 3434 C
FOREST No. 51 ARCH DRC 3435 C

1.48 mi.   0.64 mi.   0.65 mi.   0.27 mi.   0.30 mi.

0.144   0.160   0.158   0.185   0.173

LEWIS SH   ALMOND FM

114

After McCubbin and Brady, 1969

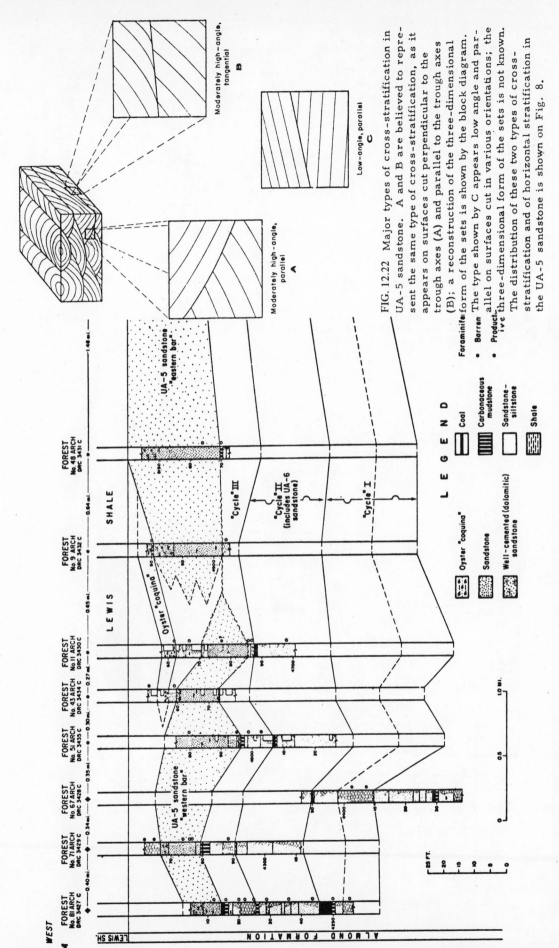

FIG. 12.22 Major types of cross-stratification in UA-5 sandstone. A and B are believed to represent the same type of cross-stratification, as it appears on surfaces cut perpendicular to the trough axes (A) and parallel to the trough axes (B); a reconstruction of the three-dimensional form of the sets is shown by the block diagram. The type shown by C appears low angle and parallel on surfaces cut in various orientations; the three-dimensional form of the sets is not known. The distribution of these two types of cross-stratification and of horizontal stratification in the UA-5 sandstone is shown on Fig. 8.

FIG. 12.23 Lithology and stratigraphy of upper Almond Formation, Patrick Draw area. Lithology is based on core studies. Distribution of samples analyzed for Foraminifera is shown beside columns; types and relative abundances of Foraminifera tabulated in Appendix II. Location of section shown on Figs. 3 and 4.

After McCubbin and Brady, 1969

115

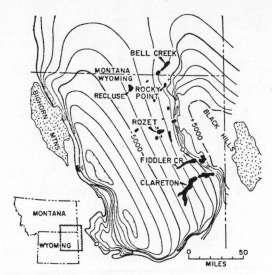

FIG. 12.24 Index map of Powder River basin, Wyoming and Montana, showing location of some principal oil fields in Muddy Sandstone, including Bell Creek field. Structural datum is on top of Dakota sandstone. C. I. = 1,000 ft.

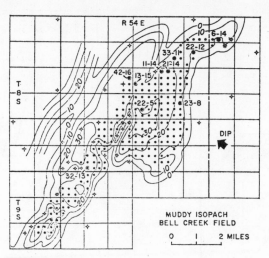

FIG. 12.25 Isopach map of Muddy Sandstone at Bell Creek field showing gross thickness of Muddy. C. I. = 10 ft. Core samples were obtained from numbered wells. Modified from McGregor and Biggs (1968, Fig. 9).

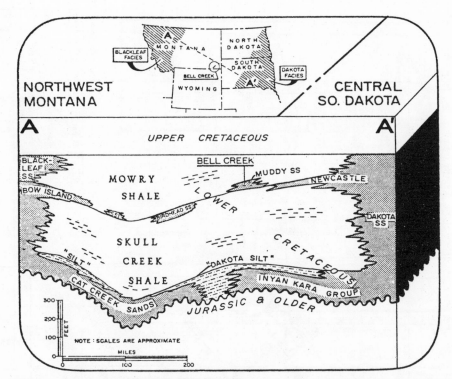

FIG. 12.26 Diagrammatic northwest-southeast cross section of Lower Cretaceous rocks from northwest Montana to central South Dakota.

After McGregor and Biggs, 1968

116

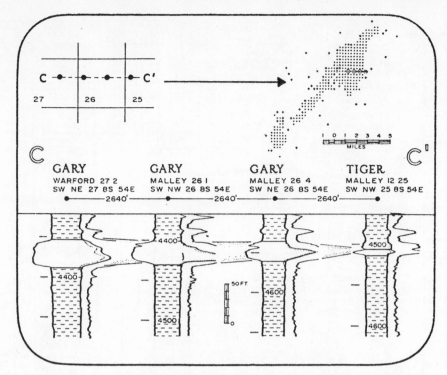

FIG. 12.27 West-east cross section of Muddy Sandstone across eastern part of Bell Creek field, showing eastward thinning of reservoir rock.

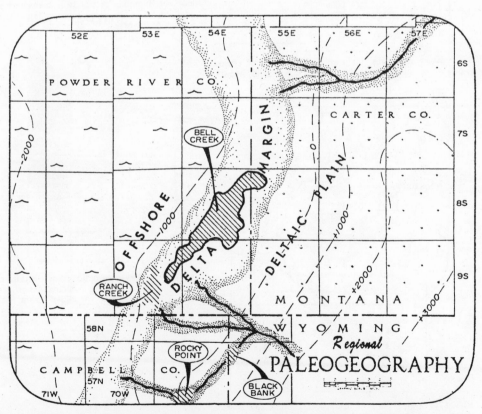

FIG. 12.28 Depths of Muddy Sandstone paleoenvironments in Bell Creek and Rocky Point areas. Modified from Figures 16 and 22. Structural datum is top of Muddy Sandstone. CI = 1,000 ft.

After McGregor and Biggs, 1968

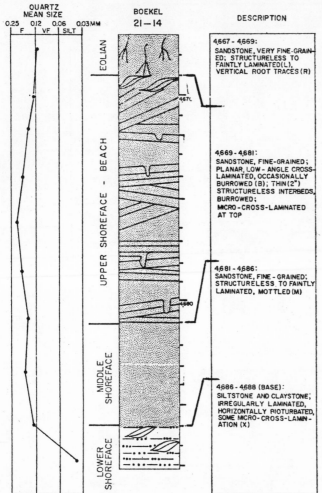

FIG. 12.29 Sedimentary structures, textures, and lithology of typical barrier-bar reservoir sediments in well 6–14, Bell Creek field, Montana.

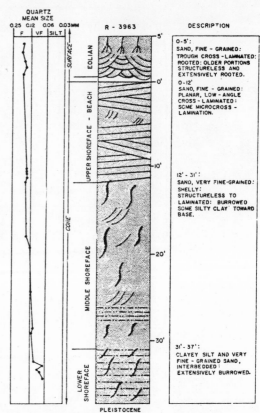

FIG. 12.30 Sedimentary structures, textures, and lithology of typical barrier island sediments in core R-3963 from Galveston Island. Eolian sediments were not cored; eolian section was measured close to original core site in order to complete vertical sequence of environments.

FIG. 12.31 Index map of northwest Gulf of Mexico showing location of Galveston Island (X indicates location of core R–3963, illustrated in Fig. 3).

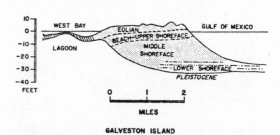

GALVESTON ISLAND

FIG. 12.32 Diagrammatic cross section of Galveston Island, Texas, showing principal environments of barrier island complex. Modified from Bernard et al. (1962, Fig. 12, p. 204).

Davies, Ethridge & Berg, 1971

118

BARRIER ISLAND (SHORELINE) AND ASSOCIATED ENVIRONMENTS

Quaternary Environments

Bernard, H. A. and LeBlanc, R. J. Sr., 1965, Resume of the Quaternary Geology of the Northwestern Gulf of Mexico: in The Quaternary of the United States, Princeton Univ. Press, Princeton, N. J., p. 154-159.

Bernard, H. A., Major, C. F., Parrott, B. S., and LeBlanc, R. J., Sr., 1970, Recent sediments of southeast Texas: Texas Bur. Econ. Geol. Guidebook no. 11, Austin, Texas.

Curray, J. R. and Moore, D. G., 1964, Holocene regressive littoral sand, Costa de Nayarit, Mexico: in Van Straaten, L. M. J. U. (ed.), Deltaic and Shallow Marine Deposits, Elsevier, Amsterdam, p. 76-82.

Curray, J. R. and Moore, D. G., 1964, Pleistocene deltaic progradation of continental terrace, Costa de Nayarit, Mexico: in Van Andel, R. H. and Shor, G. G., Jr., (eds.), Marine Geology of the Gulf of California, Amer. Assoc, Petrol. Geol. Memoir, p. 193-215.

Dickinson, K. A., Berryhill, H. L., Jr., and Holmes, C. W., 1972, Criteria for recognizing ancient barrier coastlines: Soc. Econ. Paleo. Min. Sp. Pub. no. 16, p. 192-214.

*Hoyt, J. H., 1967, Barrier Island Formation: Geol. Soc. Amer. Bull., v. 78, p. 1125-1136.

Discussion of Above Paper

Cooke, C. W., 1968, Barrier Island Formation: Discussion: Geol. Soc. Amer. Bull., v. 79, p. 945-947.

Fisher, J. J., 1968, Barrier Island Formation: Discussion: Geol. Soc. Amer. Bull., v. 79, p. 1421-1431.

Hoyt, J. H., 1969, Chenier vs. barrier, genetic and stratigraphic distinction: Amer. Assoc. Petrol. Geol. Bull., v. 53, no. 2, p. 299-306.

*Hoyt, J. H. and Henry, R. J., Jr., 1967, Influence of island migration on barrier island sedimentation: Geol. Soc. Amer. Bull., v. 78, p. 77-86.

*LeBlanc, R. J. Sr., 1972, Geometry of sandstone reservoir bodies: Amer. Assoc, Petrol. Geol. Memoir 18, p. 133-177 (also in AAPG Reprint Series No. 7).

Price, W. A., 1951, Barrier island not offshore bar: Science, v. 113, p. 487-488.

Schwartz, M. L. (ed.), 1973, Barrier islands: Benchmark Papers in Geology, Dowden, Hutchinson and Ross, Inc., Stroudsburg, Pa.

_____, (ed.), 1972, Spits and bars: Benchmark Papers in Geology, Dowden, Hutchinson and Ross, Inc., Stroudsburg, Pa.

Shepard, F. P., 1960, Gulf coast barriers: in Recent Sediments, Northwest Gulf of Mexico, 1951-58, Amer. Assoc. Petrol. Geol., Tulsa, p. 197-220.

Shoreline Deposits - Ancient

Berg, R. R. and Davies, D. K., 1968, Origin of Lower Cretaceous muddy sandstone at Bell Creek, Montana: Amer. Assoc. Petrol. Geol. Bull., v. 52, no. 10. p. 1888-1898.

*Davies, D. K., Ethridge, F. G. and Berg, R. R., 1971, Recognition of barrier environments: Amer. Assoc. Petrol. Geol. Bull., v. 55, no. 4, p. 550-565.

Hollenshead, C. T. and Pritchard, R. L., 1961, Geometry of producing Mesaverde sandstones, San Juan Basin: in Amer. Assoc. Petrol. Geol. Book - Geometry of Sandstone Bodies, p. 98-118.

Hoyt, J. H., 1967, Pleistocene shoreline sediments in coastal Georgia: Deposition and modification: Science, v. 155, no. 3769, p. 1541-1543.

Howard, J. D., 1972, Trace fossils as criteria for recognizing shorelines in stratigraphic record: Soc. Econ. Paleo. and Min. Sp. Pub. 16, p. 215-225.

Klein, G. deV., 1974, Estimating water depths from analysis of barrier island and deltaic sedimentary sequences: Geology, v. 2, no. 8, p. 409-412.

*Land, C. B., Jr., 1972, Stratigraphy of Fox Hills Sandstone and associated formations, Rock Springs uplift and Wamsutter arch area, Sweetwater County, Wyoming: a shoreline-estuary sandstone model for the Late Cretaceous: Colorado School of Mines Quart., v. 67, no. 2, 69 p.

*McCubbin, D. G. and Brady, M. J., 1969, Depositional environment of the Almond reservoirs, Patrick Draw Field, Wyoming: The Mountain Geologist, v. 6, no. 1. p. 3-26.

McGregor, A. A. and Biggs, C. A., 1968, Bell Creek Field, Montana: a rich stratigraphic trap: Amer. Assoc. Petrol. Geol. Bull., v. 52, no. 10, p. 1869-1887.

Sabins, F. F., Jr., 1963, Anatomy of stratigraphic traps, Bisti Oil field, New Mexico: Amer. Assoc. Petrol. Geol. Bull., v. 47, p. 193-228.

*Weimer, R. J., 1966, Time-stratigraphic analysis and petroleum accumulation, Patrick Draw Field, Wyoming: Amer. Assoc. Petrol. Geol. Bull., v. 50 no. 10, p. 2150-2175.

Weimer, R. J. and Land, C. B., Jr., 1975, Maestrichtian deltaic and inter-deltaic shoreline deposits, Upper Cretaceous, Rocky Mountain region: Geol. Assoc. Can. Sp. Paper on Cretaceous (in press).

OUTLINE FOR LECTURE 10
(13)

DELTAIC VS INTERDELTAIC (OR DELTA MARGIN) ENVIRONMENTS

1. Coastal plain and shallow marine environments and processes.
   a) To determine position of a vertical section in overall depositional
      system, one must be able to distinguish between deltaic and inter-
      deltaic areas of sedimentation.
   b) Importance of evaluation of the overall lighologies and establishing
      genetic units in a regressive sequence involving marine silts and
      clays (offshore), overlain by marine sands (nearshore and shoreline),
      and capped by clays, silts, sands, coals (coastal plain).
   c) Coastal plain deposits: similarity of processes filling open bays in
      deltaic plain setting and filling lagoons in interdeltaic coastal plain
      setting; therefore, genetic units are similar.
      1) Crevasse-splay subdelta filling open bay; example, Cubits Gap and
         Bay Rondo, Mississippi Delta (Fig. 13.1); also processes and litholo-
         gies of subdelta shown by Figs. 13.2, 13.3.
      2) Minor delta filling in lagoon (lagoonal delta); example, Guadalupe
         Delta - San Antonio Bay (lagoon) Central Texas Coast (Figs. 13.4-
         13.8.
      3) Differences: Case 1 (above) has no well defined shoreline deposit
         between site of deposition and shallow marine (no high energy zone
         yielding porous and permeable sand); Case 2 has barrier bar (high
         energy) between low energy lagoon and shelf deposits.
   d) Tidal-dominated, coastal plain deposit: tidal channels (estuaries),
      tidal flats, marsh or swamp; deposits are generally on delta margin or
      in interdeltaic areas.
      1) Migrating tidal channels may leave sheet-like channel sand with scour
         base. During regression, the top or all of barrier bar may be
         destroyed. Modern example: Niger Delta (Figs. 13.10-13.16).
      2) Associated tidal flats and salt marsh marginal to tidal channels in
         progradational sequence. Example: Netherlands and German coast,
         (Figs. 13.18-13.20).
   e) Shoreline deposits of major delta vs interdeltaic areas (Fig. 13.9):
      Compare beach - shore face processes and deposits (Lecture 12, Figs.
      13.26, 13.28, Table 13.3) with delta front processes and deposits

(Lecture 11, also 13.24, 13.25, Table 13.1).
  f) Shelf deposits influenced by deltaic vs interdeltaic sedimentation: compare lithologies of prodelta marine shales with shelf shales (offshore from barrier island).
2. Difficulty in distinguishing between deltaic and some interdeltaic deposits in high energy coastal areas (high- destructive wave and tide deltas of Scott, Fig. 11.7). Example: Rhine River, Netherlands Coast, Figs. 13.17, 13.18.
3. Ancient example of vertical sequence of <u>genetic units</u> of deltaic vs inter-deltaic setting: Maestrichtian, Upper Cretaceous, Rocky Mountain Region.
  a) Deltaic setting: Pierre, Fox Hills, Laramie Formations, Golden, Area, Colorado; (Figs. 13.21-13-25, 13.29, Tables 13.1, 13.2, 13.4).
  b) Interdeltaic setting: Lewis, Fox Hills, Lance Formations, Rock Springs area, Wyoming: (Figs. 13.26-13.28, Table 13.3).
4. Ancient example of lagoonal delta deposits, Almond Formation, Wyoming, (Figs. 12.16, 12.17, 12.20, 12.23). Thin distributary sandstones which are oil-productive are labeled UA-6.
5. Ancient example of crevasse splay subdelta deposits, Laramie Formation, Upper Cretaceous, Golden Area (Fig. 13.29, Table 13.4)
6. Petroleum exploration of lagoonal and crevasse splay deltas.
  a) Small deltas are like major deltas (Lecture 11) except they are lower energy systems building into shallow bodies of water with low energy (i.e. bays or lagoons).
  b) Setting of reservoir sands same as major delta: distributary channel, distributary mouth bar, delta front. However, thickness of reservoir sands generally 10 feet or less in thickness with little or no effective porosity and permeability. Narrow distributary channel probably has best reservoir quality.
  c) In the case of the crevasse delta, recognition of feature may indicate proximity to major distributary channel reservoir. Recognition of lagoonal delta setting may suggest barrier bar in seaward direction.
7. Setting of coal and uranium deposits similar to that discussed in Lectures 11 and 12.
8. Examples of crevasse splay subdelta and lagoonal delta available for study during seminar: Outcrop - "J" Sandstone; Laramie Formation; Cores - "J" Sandstone, Peoria Field, Colorado; Almond Formation, Patrick Draw Field, Wyoming.

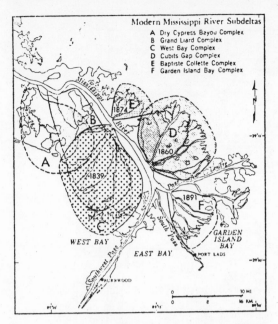

The subdeltas of the modern Mississippi River.
After Coleman and Gagliano, 1964.

a

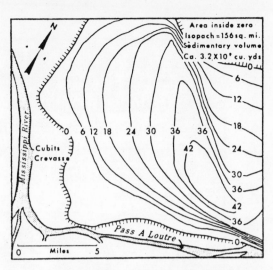

Isopach map of sedimentary fill in Bay Rondo,
Mississippi delta, between 1873 and 1968. Thicknesses in
feet. See Text and Figure 8.

b

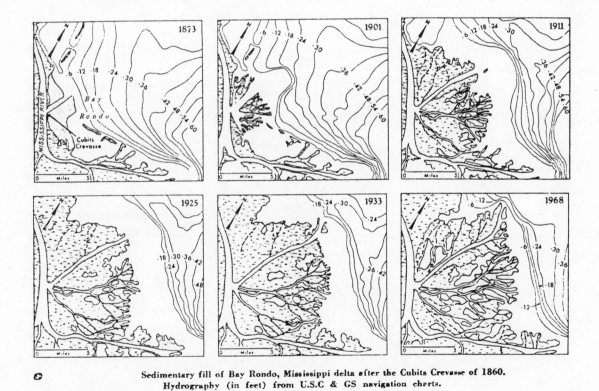

c Sedimentary fill of Bay Rondo, Mississippi delta after the Cubits Crevasse of 1860.
Hydrography (in feet) from U.S.C & GS navigation charts.

FIG. 13.1 Example of a subdelta crevasse-splay deposit from modern Mississippi River delta
that formed after Cubits Crevasse of 1860. From Morgan, 1970, p. 113, 115.

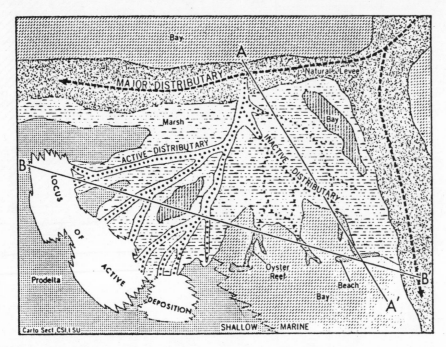

FIG. 13.2   Areal distribution of principal depositional units, crevasse splay facies.   From Coleman and Gagliano (1964).

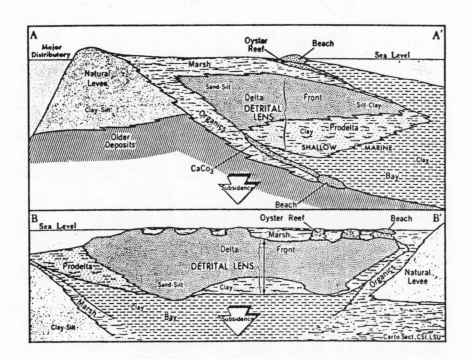

FIG. 13.3   Cross sections of depositional units, in crevasse splay shown in Fig. 16.   From Coleman and Gagliano (1964).

After Fisher, et al., 1969

124

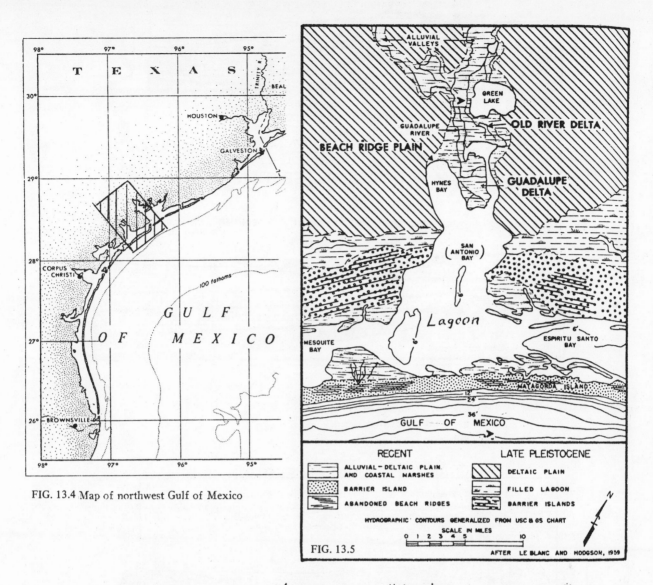

FIG. 13.4 Map of northwest Gulf of Mexico

FIG. 13.5

RECENT

ALLUVIAL-DELTAIC PLAIN
AND COASTAL MARSHES

BARRIER ISLAND

ABANDONED BEACH RIDGES

LATE PLEISTOCENE

DELTAIC PLAIN

FILLED LAGOON

BARRIER ISLANDS

HYDROGRAPHIC CONTOURS GENERALIZED FROM USC & GS CHART

SCALE IN MILES
0 1 2 3 4 5   10

AFTER LE BLANC AND HODGSON, 1959

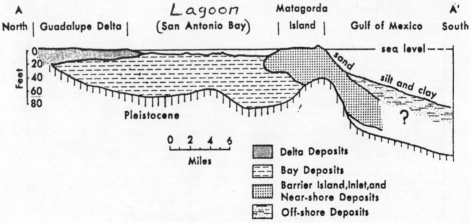

Delta Deposits

Bay Deposits

Barrier Island, Inlet, and
Near-shore Deposits

Off-shore Deposits

FIG. 13.6 Geologic setting of Guadalupe delta showing relationship of late Pleistocene sediments to Holocene sediments and a generalized interpretation after Shepard and Moore (1955) of cross section from Guadalupe delta to Gulf of Mexico.

After Donaldson, et al., 1970

125

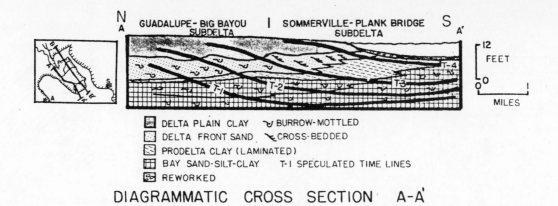

DIAGRAMMATIC CROSS SECTION A-A'

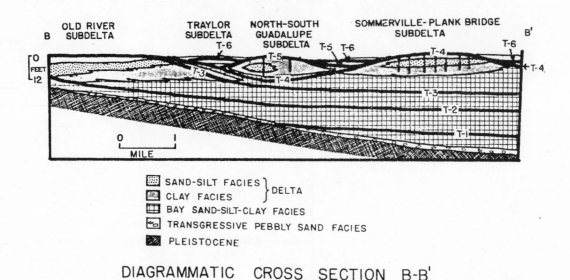

DIAGRAMMATIC CROSS SECTION B-B'

FIG. 13.7 Diagrammatic cross section A-A' shows Guadalupe delta prograding into an increasingly shoaling bay. Deposition in deeper water initially resulted in thicker delta-front sands, slower progradation, and more abundant burrow mottling than in more rapidly prograding Sommerville-Plank Bridge subdelta. Bay presently transgressive at southern end of delta. Diagrammatic cross section B-B' shows lateral shifting of subdeltas with time. Time lines are speculative.

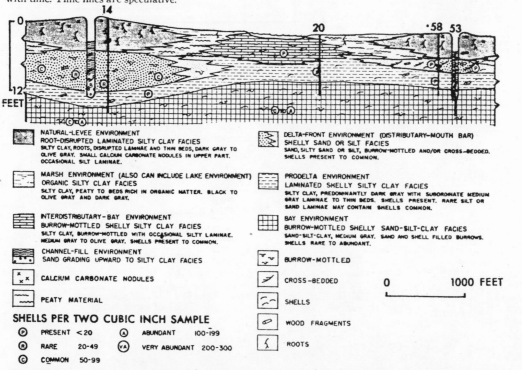

FIG. 13.8 Diagrammatic cross section illustrating facies of Guadalupe delta. Selected cores, which are representative of facies, are located only approximately on cross section.

After Donaldson, et al., 1970

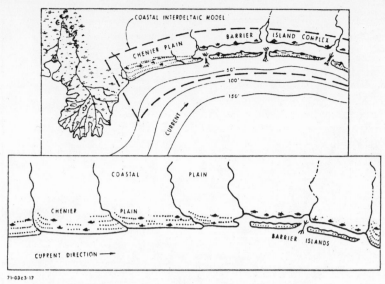

After LeBlanc, 1972

FIG. 13.9 General setting and characteristics of coastal-interdeltaic model of clastic sedimentation.

After Oomkens, 1974

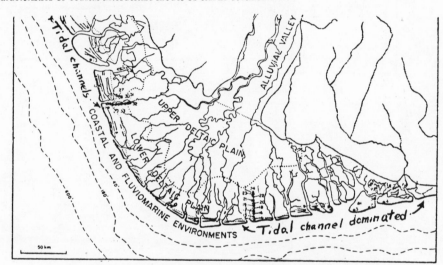

FIG. 13.10 Late Quaternary Niger Delta. Corehole location map.

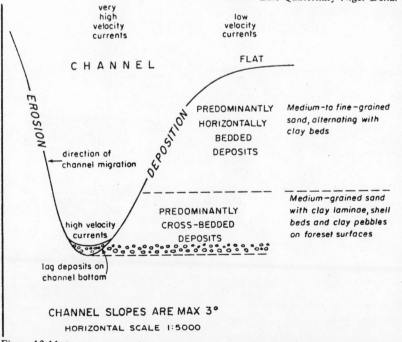

Figure 13.11 Cross section of a migrating estuary channel, Haringvliet, Netherlands (after Oomkens and Terwindt, 1960).

127

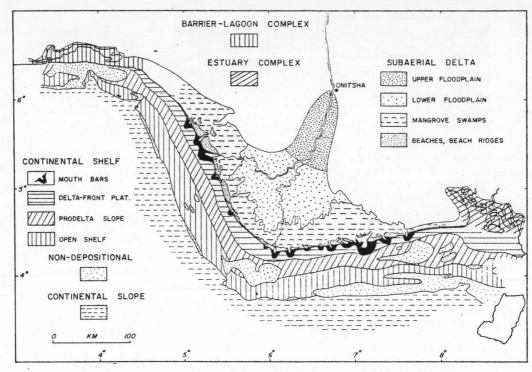

FIG. 13.12 Sedimentary environments of Niger delta area. See also Figure 1 and Table I.

After Allen, 1965

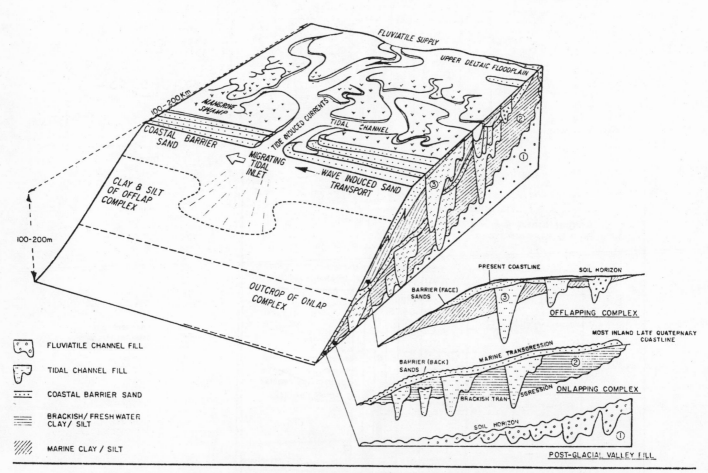

FIG. 13.13 Lithofacies relations in the Late Quaternary Niger Delta.

After Oomkens, 1974

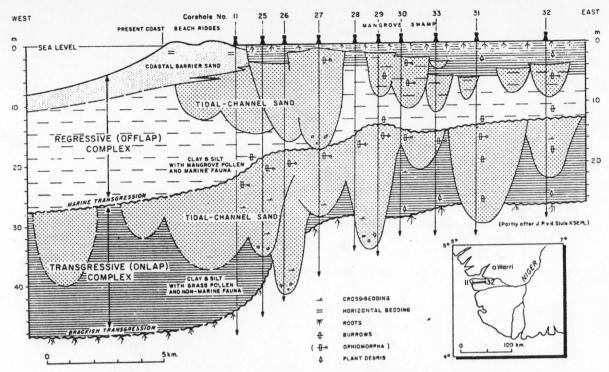

FIG. 13.14 Transgressive and regressive sequences in the Late Quaternary Niger Delta.

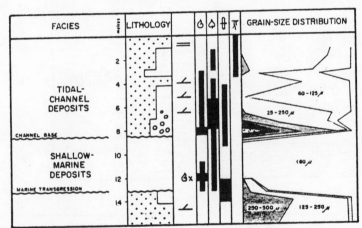

FIG. 13.15 Regressive sequence with tidal channel-fill sand member. Corehole 4 (for core photographs see Fig. 16). For key see Fig. 4.

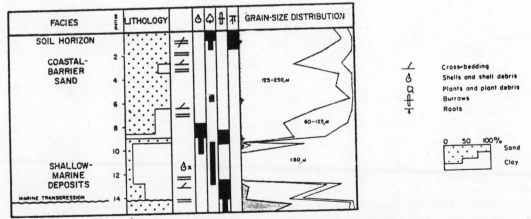

FIG. 13.16 Regressive sequence with coastal-barrier sand member. Corehole 1 (for core photographs see Fig. 15). For key see Fig. 4.

After Oomkens, 1974

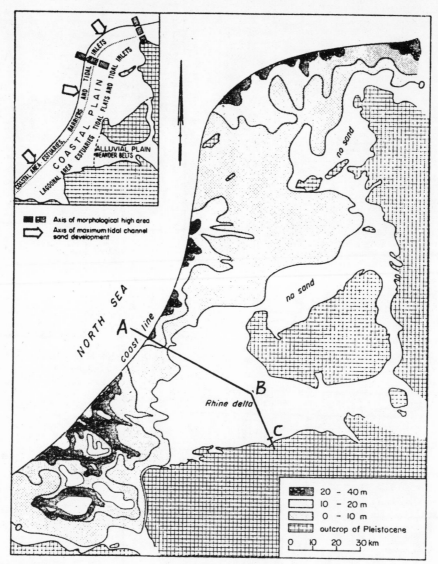

FIG. 13.17 Distribution of recent tidal channel-fill sands in the lower coastal plain of the Netherlands. After Oomkens, 1974

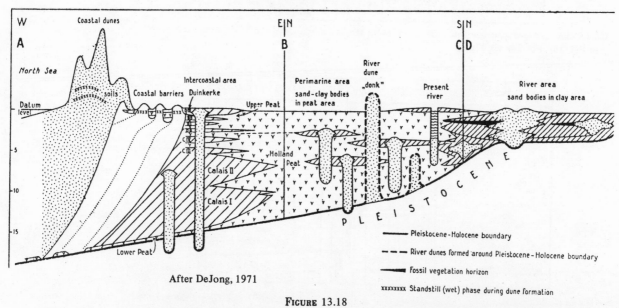

After DeJong, 1971

FIGURE 13.18
Schematic representation of a cross-section through the Holocene formations of The Netherlands.

130

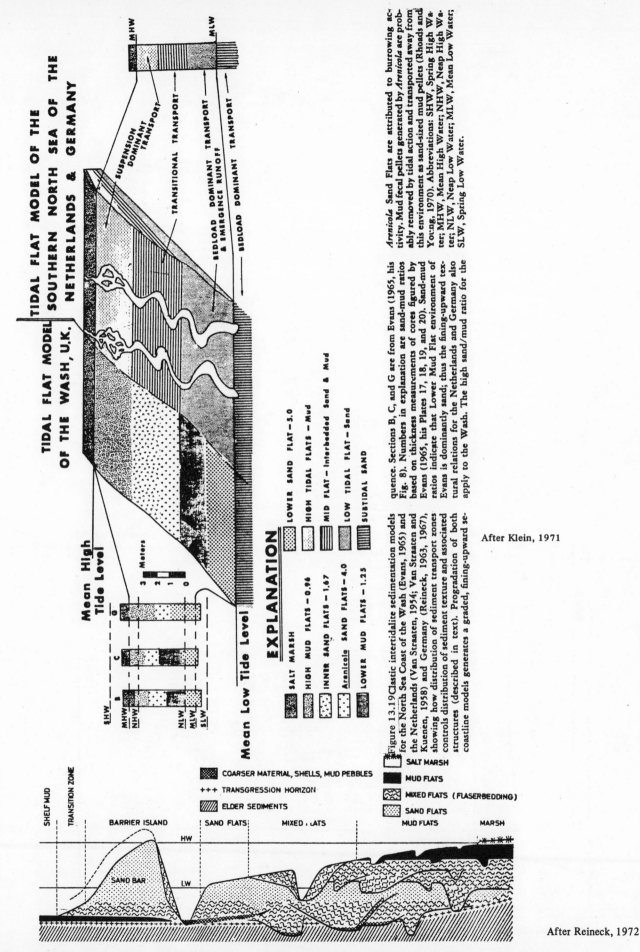

TIDAL FLAT MODEL
OF THE WASH, U.K.

TIDAL FLAT MODEL OF THE
SOUTHERN NORTH SEA OF THE
NETHERLANDS & GERMANY

SUSPENSION DOMINANT TRANSPORT

TRANSITIONAL TRANSPORT

BEDLOAD DOMINANT TRANSPORT & EMERGENCE RUNOFF

BEDLOAD DOMINANT TRANSPORT

Mean High Tide Level

3 Meters
2
1
0

Mean Low Tide Level

SHW
MHW
NHW

MLW
MLW
SLW

B   C   G

EXPLANATION

	SALT MARSH
	HIGH MUD FLATS — 0.96
	INNER SAND FLATS — 1.67
	Arenicola SAND FLATS — 4.0
	LOWER MUD FLATS — 1.25

	LOWER SAND FLAT — 5.0
	HIGH TIDAL FLATS — Mud
	MID FLAT — Interbedded Sand & Mud
	LOW TIDAL FLAT — Sand
	SUBTIDAL SAND

Figure 13.19 Clastic interdidalite sedimentation models for the North Sea Coast of the Wash (Evans, 1965) and the Netherlands (Van Straaten, 1954; Van Straaten and Kuenen, 1958) and Germany (Reineck, 1963, 1967), showing how distribution of sediment transport zones controls distribution of sediment texture and associated structures (described in text). Progradation of both coastline models generates a graded, fining-upward sequence. Sections B, C, and G are from Evans (1965, his Fig. 8). Numbers in explanation are sand-mud ratios based on thickness measurements of cores figured by Evans (1965, his Plates 17, 18, 19, and 20). Sand-mud ratios indicate that Lower Mud Flat environment of Evans is dominantly sand; thus the fining-upward textural relations for the Netherlands and Germany also apply to the Wash. The high sand/mud ratio for the

Arenicola Sand Flats are attributed to burrowing activity. Mud fecal pellets generated by *Arenicola* are probably removed by tidal action and transported away from this environment as sand-sized mud pellets (Rhoads and Young, 1970). Abbreviations: SHW, Spring High Water; MHW, Mean High Water; NHW, Neap High Water; NLW, Neap Low Water; MLW, Mean Low Water; SLW, Spring Low Water.

After Klein, 1971

	COARSER MATERIAL, SHELLS, MUD PEBBLES
+++	TRANSGRESSION HORIZON
	ELDER SEDIMENTS

	SALT MARSH
	MUD FLATS
	MIXED FLATS (FLASERBEDDING)
	SAND FLATS

SHELF MUD   TRANSITION ZONE   BARRIER ISLAND   SAND FLATS   MIXED FLATS   MUD FLATS   MARSH

HW

SAND BAR

LW

After Reineck, 1972

FIG. 13.20 Vertical sequence of slowly deposited progradational deposits reworked by meandering channels. The lower part (subtidal zone) is built of channel deposits. Left side is open sea.

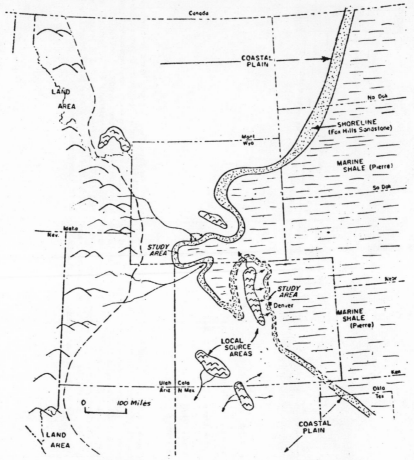

FIG. 13.21—Maestrichtian deltaic and inter-deltaic areas of sedimentation.

After Weimer and Land, 1975

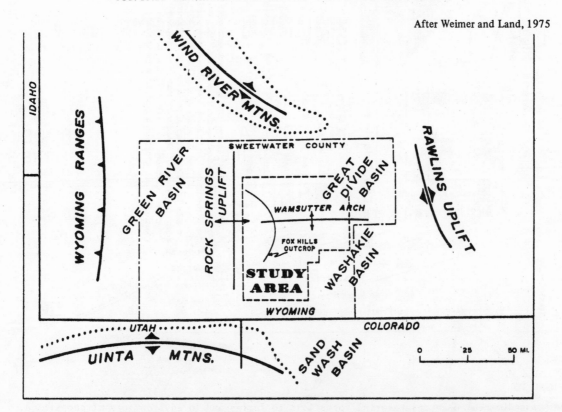

FIG. 13.22 Location map showing major tectonic features of southwestern Wyoming and adjacent states.

After Land, 1972

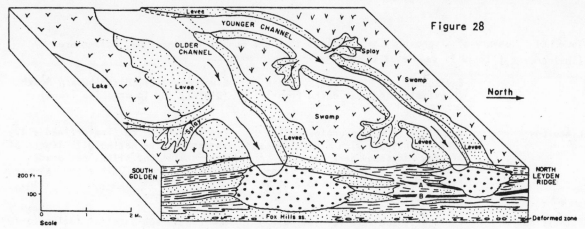

Figure 28

FIG. 13.23   Summary sketch diagram of relationships observed in lower Laramie Formation from Leyden Ridge to Golden (Modified after Camacho, 1969).

FIG. 13.24   Sketch showing reconstruction of delta-front environments inferred to be present to the east during the time of lower Laramie deposition in Golden-Leyden area.

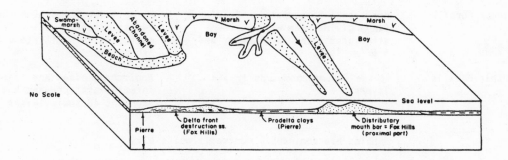

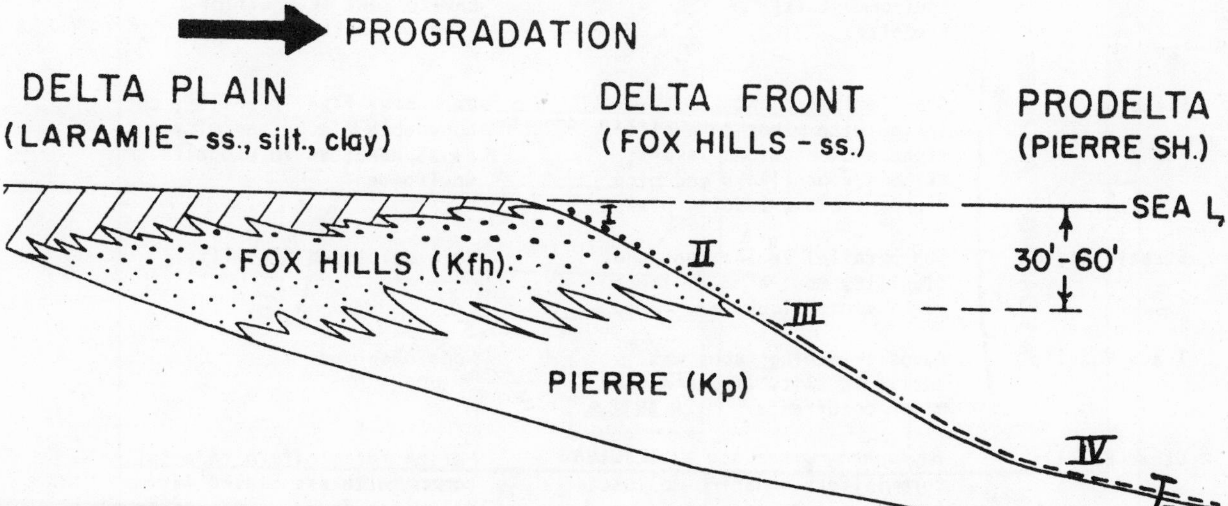

PROGRADATION

DELTA PLAIN
(LARAMIE - ss., silt., clay)

DELTA FRONT
(FOX HILLS - ss.)

PRODELTA
(PIERRE SH.)

SEA L.

30'-60'

FOX HILLS (Kfh)

PIERRE (Kp)

I
II
III
IV
T_2
T_1

FIG. 13.25

Delta sedimentation model relating formations to facies and to environments of deposition.
After Weimer, 1973

133

Table 13.1   Summary of diagnostic characteristics of the Fox Hills Sandstone, Golden area (Environment I to IV is sea level to neritic).

	Environment I, Distributary Mouth (Proximal) (or upper delta front)	Environment II, Distributary Mouth (Distal) (or lower delta front)
Lithology	Tan fine- to medium-grained well sorted sandstone with minor layers of gray micaceous carbonaceous silty shale; calcareous and iron-cemented concretions up to 2 ft in diameter.	Tan very fine- to fine-grained silty sandstone alternating with layers of gray shale[1] and siltstone; gradational upward to unit above; abundant mica and carbonaceous flecks along bedding planes.
Stratification	Dominantly sub-parallel laminations with minor ripple micro-cross-lamination. Some sets of trough cross strata up to 2 ft thick. Deformational "ball and pillow" structure are common.	Dominantly sub-parallel laminations with some ripple microcross-lamination. Small scale deformational structures common in thin layers; occasional large scale slump structures; many cone-in-cone layers of calcium carbonate.
Trace Fossils	Not abundant; suspension feeding fauna giving rare wall burrow structures ½ in. in diameter and 4-6 in. long.	No well-developed bioturbate textures; deposit-feeding fauna was active in thin siltstone or sandstone layers.
Other Fossils	Sparse *Haplophragmoides* in shale layers.	*Haplophragmoides* and associated foraminifera; present but not abundant in shale layers.

[1]Shales are dominantly montmorillonite clay

Table 13.2   Summary of diagnostic characteristics of the upper Pierre Shale, Golden, Colorado.

	Environment III Prodelta	Environment IV shelf or deeper neritic
Lithology	Gray laminated and fissile shale[1] with minor thin siltstone and sandstone layers; carbonaceous flecks and mica abundant along bedding planes.	Dark gray fissile shale[1]; carbonaceous flecks and mica not as abundant as in prodelta environment.
Stratification	Sub-parallel laminations and fissility most common; large scale slump blocks are rare.	Well developed fissility.
Trace Fossils	Deposit-feeding fauna was active in silty layers as minor occurrence.	None observed.
Other Fossils	*Haplophragmoides* and associated foraminifers. Marine molluscan fauna rare; occasional ammonite.	Marine foraminifera rare to common with associated marine molluscan fauna. *Sphenodiscus coahuilites, Inoceramus fibrosus* and *Baculites clinolobatus.*

[1]Shales are dominantly montmorillonite clay   After Weimer, 1973

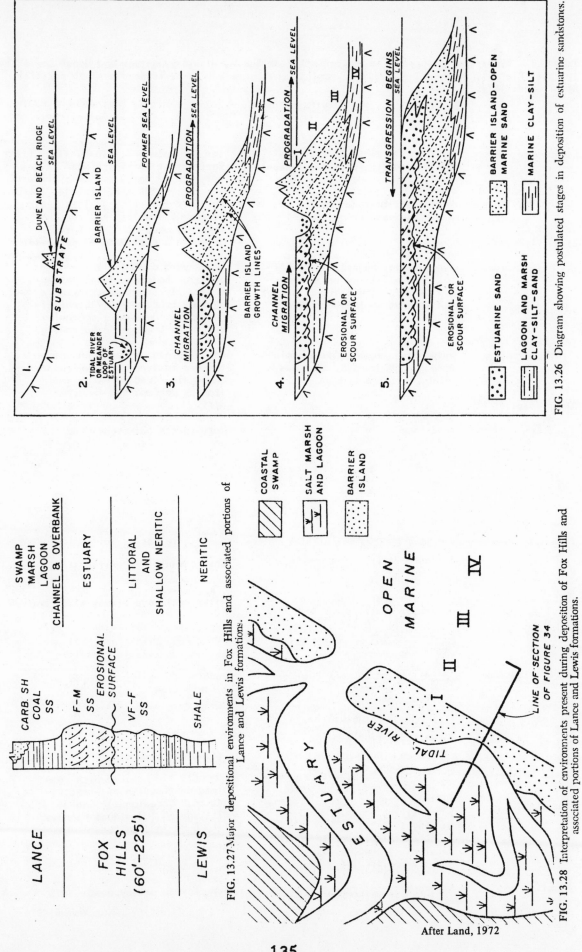

FIG. 13.26 Diagram showing postulated stages in deposition of estuarine sandstones.

FIG. 13.27 Major depositional environments in Fox Hills and associated portions of Lance and Lewis formations.

FIG. 13.28 Interpretation of environments present during deposition of Fox Hills and associated portions of Lance and Lewis formations.

After Land, 1972

135

Table 13.3   Summary of diagnostic characteristics of the Fox Hills Sandstone and Upper Lewis Shale
(= upper Pierre), Rock Springs uplift, Wyoming (Environment I to IV is sea level to neritic).
After Land, 1972.

	Environment I--Foreshore (beach)	Environment II--Shoreface
Lithology	Very fine- to fine-grained, well sorted sandstone.	Very fine- to fine-grained sandstone. Grain size and sorting increase upward. Thin interbeds of shale and siltstone near base.
Stratification	Sub-parallel bedded. Stratification has 1-3 degrees primary dip seaward, and exhibits slight wedging-out in landward direction.	Lower part dominantly sub-parallel bedded. Upper part dominantly cross-stratified in shallow trough sets. Stratification in lower part commonly destroyed by organic burrowing.
Trace Fossils	Suspension-feeding fauna dominated by *Ophiomorpha*. Burrows of *Arenicolites* common.	Deposit-feeding fauna and bioturbate textures in lower part. Suspension-feeding fauna dominated by *Ophiomorpha* in upper part.
Fossils	None found.	Very sparse pelecypods and ammonites. Few abraded oyster shells.

	Environment III-Sub-Shoreface	Environment IV--Neritic (Lewis Shale)
Lithology	Very fine-grained sandstone. Interbeds of siltstone and silty shale. Grain size increases upward in vertical sequence.	Silty shale and clayey siltstone
Stratification	Largely thin- to very thin-bedded. Sub-parallel stratification dominant. Minor ripple lamination and low-angle cross-stratification. Symmetrical ripple marks common.	Bedding commonly destroyed by bioturbation.
Trace Fossils	*Rhizocorallium*, miniature form of *Ophiomorpha*(?), and sand-filled burrows common. Trails, burrows, and organic markings on bedding surfaces. Thin (½- to 4 in.-thick) bioturbate zones parallel to bedding. *Ophiomorpha* and *Arenicolites* very sparse.	Commonly bioturbated with complete destruction of stratification. Occasionally can distinguish individual burrows 1 to 6 mm in diameter.
Fossils	Very sparse pelecypods and ammonites.	Very sparse pelecypods.

After Weimer, 1973

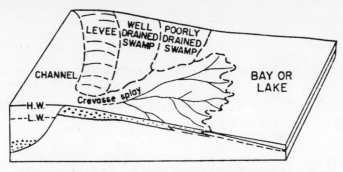

LARAMIE ENVIRONMENTS OF DEPOSITION

FIG. 13.29 Relationship of channel margin environments of Fig. 14 to crevasse splay deposits of the Laramie Formation.

Table 13.4 Summary of diagnostic characteristics of the Laramie Formation, Golden, Colorado.

	Channel[1]	Swamp well-drained	Swamp poorly drained	Lacustrine	Splay sandstone
Lithology	Gray to brown fine to coarse-grained sandstone with clay clasts near base. Fining upward grain size. Large-scale load casts along base. Clay grains common. Scour base.	Light gray and pink kaolinite claystones with iron-rich concretionary layers 1 to 3 in. thick.	Dark gray to black kaolinite claystone], carbonaceous shale and thin coal seams.	Medium to dark gray claystone and organic rich shale with minor siltstone and very fine-grained sandstone layers.	Gray to brown fine- to medium grained sandstone. Texture fining upward; scour base near main channel; sharp or transitional base away from channel. Sandstone thins and becomes finer-grained away from main channel.
Stratification	Trough cross strata with sets up to 2 ft in thickness in lower part. Ripple microcross-lamination in upper part.	Generally, massive appearing; "clay skin" fracturing by root system expansion is common.	Laminations of bedding present in carbonaceous rich strata.	Generally well laminated or bedded.	Dominantly ripple microcross-lamination; trough cross-stratification common in lower part.
Fossils	Log and leaf imprints common along base.	Occasional carbonized plant fragment or imprint; root systems.	Carbonized plant remains and imprints; root systems	Leaf and plant fragment imprints.	Numerous log imprints as "log jams" common along base; palm fronds and leaf imprints in upper part.

[1]Levees have not been specifically identified in outcrop sections in Golden area.

137

DELTAIC PLAIN ENVIRONMENTS

Channel - Levee - Splay Delta - Bay - Swamp - Marsh

Bedwell, J. L., 1974, Textural parameters of clastic rocks from borehole measurements and their application in determining depositional environments: PhD dissertation, Colorado School of Mines, T-1621, (unpub.) 215 p.

Carloss, J. C., 1974, Depositional environments from borehole measurements, Lower Cretaceous, Peoria Field and adjacent area, Arapahoe County, Colorado: MSc thesis (unpub.), Colorado School of Mines, Golden, Colo.

Coleman, J. M. and Gagliano, S. M., 1964, Cyclic sedimentation in the Mississippi River deltaic plain: Gulf Coast Assoc. Geol. Soc. Trans., v. 14, p. 67-80.

*Coleman, J. M., Gagliano, S. M., and Webb, J. E., 1964, Minor sedimentary structures in a prograding distributary: Marine Geol., v. 1, p. 240-258.

Fisk, H. N., et al., 1954, Sedimentary framework of the modern Mississippi delta: Jour. Sed. Petrology, v. 24, p. 76-99.

MacMillan, L. T., 1974, Stratigraphy of the South Platte Formation (Lower Cretaceous), Morrison--Weaver Gulch area, Jefferson County, Colorado: Colorado School of Mines MSc Thesis T-1626, (unpub.).

Morgan, J. P., 1970, Deltas--A resume: Jour. Geol. Educ., v. 18, no. 3, p. 107-117.

*Weimer, R. J., 1973, A guide to uppermost Cretaceous stratigraphy, central Front Range, Colorado: deltaic sedimentation, growth faulting and early Laramide crustal movement: The Mountain Geologist, v. 10, no. 3, p. 53-97.

*_____, 1975, Maestrichtian deltaic and interdeltaic sedimentation, Rocky Mountain region in the United States: Geol. Assoc. Canada Sp. Pub. on Cretaceous (in press).

Weimer, R. J. and Land, C. B., 1972, Field guide to Dakota Group (Cretaceous) stratigraphy, Golden-Morrison area, Colorado: The Mountain Geologist, v. 9, nos. 2-3 p. 241-267.

Welder, F. A., 1959, Processes of deltaic sedimentation in the lower Mississippi River: Louisiana State Univ. Coastal Studies Inst. Tech. Report 12, 90 p.

INTERDELTAIC COASTAL PLAIN ENVIRONMENTS

Lagoons - Lagoonal Delta - Marsh

Ayaia-Castanares, A. A. and Phleger, F. B,(eds.), 1969, Coastal Lagoons, A Symposium: Universidad Nacional Autonoma de Mexico, Mexico City, 686 p. (espec. Phleger, p. 5-25).

*Donaldson, A. C., Martin, R. H., and Kanes, W. H., 1970, Holocene Guadalupe Delta of Texas Gulf Coast: in Soc. Econ. Paleo. Min. Sp. Pub. 15, p. 107-137.

FitzGerald, D. M. and Bouma, A., 1972, Consolidation studies of deltaic sediments: Gulf Coast Assoc. Geol. Soc. Trans., v. 22, p. 165-173.

Kanes, W. H., 1970, Facies and development of the Colorado River Delta in Texas in Soc. Econ. Paleo. Min. Sp. Pub. 15, p. 78-106.

Lankford, R. R. and Rogers, J. J. W., 1969, Holocene geology of the Galveston Bay area: Houston Geol. Soc., 144 p.

Oomkens, E., 1974, Lithofacies relations in the Late Quaternary Niger delta complex: Sedimentology, v. 21, p. 195-222.

Shepard, F. P. and Moore, D. G., 1955, Central Texas coast sedimentation: characteristics of sedimentary environments, recent history, and diagenesis: Amer. Assoc. Petrol. Geol. Bull., v. 39, p. 1463-1593.

Shepard, F. P. and Moore, D. G., 1960, Bays of the Central Texas coast: in Shepard, F. P. and others (eds.) Recent sediments, northwest Gulf of Mexico: Tulsa, Okla., Amer. Assoc. Petrol. Geol., p. 117-152.

Tidal Channels - Estuaries - Tidal Flats - Salt Marsh

Allen, J. R. L., 1965, Late Quaternary Niger delta and adjacent area: Sedimentary environments and lithofacies: Amer. Assoc, Petrol. Geol. Bull., v. 49, p. 547-600.

Anderson, F. E., 1973, Observations of some sedimentary processes acting on a tidal flat: Mar. Geol., v. 14, p. 101-116.

Curray, J. R., 1969, Estuaries, Lagoons, Tidal Flats and Deltas: in Stanley, D. J. (ed.), The New Concepts of Continental Margin Sedimentation, Amer. Geol. Instit., Washington, D. C., 30 p.

DeJong, L. D., 1971, The scenery of the Netherlands against the background of Holocene geology: Revue de Geographie Physique et de Geologie Dynamique (2), v. 13, p. 143-162.

*Evans, G., 1965, Intertidal flat sediments and their environments of deposition in the wash: Quart. Jour. Geol. Soc., v. 121, p. 209-245.

Guilcher, A., 1967, Origin of sediments in estuaries: in Lauff, G. H. (ed.), Estuaries: Amer. Assoc. Adv. Sci., p. 149-179.

Haven, D. S. and Morales-Alamo, R., 1972, Biodeposition as a factor in sedimentation of fine suspended solids in estuaries: Geol. Soc. Amer. Memoir 133, p. 121-130.

Klein, G. deV., 1970, Depositional and dispersal dynamics of intertidal sand bars: Jour. Sed. Petrol., v. 40, p. 1095-1127.

*_____, 1971. A sedimentary model for determining paleotidal range: Geol. Soc. Amer. Bull., v. 82, p. 2585-2592.

Land, C. B., Jr., 1972, Stratigraphy of Fox Hills Sandstone and associated formations, Rock Springs uplift and Wamsutter arch area Sweetwater County, Wyoming: a shorline estuary sandstone model for the Late Cretaceous: Colorado School of Mines Quart., v. 67, no. 2, 69 p.

Lauff, G. H. (ed.), 1967, Estuaries: Amer. Assoc. Adv. Sci., Wash., D. C., 757 p.

*MacKenzie, D. B., 1972, Tidal sand flat deposits in Lower Cretaceous Dakota Group near Denver, Colorado: The Mountain Geologist, v. 9, nos. 2-3, p. 269-277.

Meade, R. H., 1969, Landward transport of bottom sediments in estuaries of the Atlantic coastal plain: Jour. Sed. Pet., v. 39, p. 222-234.

_____, 1972, Transport and deposition of sediments in estuaries: Geol. Soc. Amer. Memoir 133, p. 91-120.

Nelson, B. W., (ed.) 1972: Environmental framework of coastal plain estuaries: Geol. Soc. Amer. Memoir 133.

Oomkens, E., 1974, Lithofacies relations in the Late Quaternary Niger delta complex: Sedimentology, v. 21, p. 195-222.

Posta, H., 1967, Sediment transport and sedimentation in the estuarine environment: in Lauff, G. H. (ed.) Estuaries: Amer. Assoc. Adv. Sci., p. 158-179.

Reineck, H. E., 1967, Layered sediments of tidal flats, beaches and shelf bottoms of the North Sea: in Lauff, G. H. (ed.), Estuaries: Amer. Assoc. Adv. Sci., p. 191-206.

_____, 1972, Tidal flats: Soc. Econ. Paleo. Min. Sp. Pub. 16, p. 146-159.

Thompson, R. W., 1968, Tidal flat sedimentation on the Colorado River delta, Northwestern Gulf of Calif.: Geol. Soc. Amer. Sp. Paper 107, 133 p.

Van Stratten, L. M. J. V. and Kuenen, Ph. H., 1958, Tidal action as a cause of clay accumulation: Jour. Sed. Petrol., v. 38, p. 406-413.

OUTLINE FOR LECTURE 11
(14)

SHALLOW WATER MARINE ENVIRONMENTS (SHELF--NERITIC)

1. Major components and terminology of systems

   a) Marine sand bodies attached to shoreline and associated with barrier
   island, deltas, capes or tidal-inlets: shore face, delta fringe
   (delta front), transgressive marine sand (LeBlanc, 1972, Fig. 14.1);
   cape-associated shoal with transverse ridges and swales (Fig. 14.3);
   tidal inlet or estuary shoals (tidal deltas?) (Fig. 14.21, 14.22).

   b) Offshore bars (may have any orientation relative to shoreline trend);
   sand ridges and swales of Swift, et al. (Fig. 14.2); sand bank of
   Nelson and Bray (Fig. 14.7); tidal current ridges of Off (Fig. 14.8);
   linear sand bank of Caston (Fig. 14.9). Terminology: central bar,
   bar margin, interbar (Exum and Harms, 1968); similarity of facies to
   foreshore, short face and shelf (Fig. 14.51). Bars may have either
   fining upward or coarsening upward grain sizes.

   c) Palimpsest sand on shelf floor (transgressive sheet sand)

   d) Bar sands overlying submarine scour surfaces.

2. Processes and genetic units (facies - lithologic associations)

   a) Complicated and diverse: normal and storm-generated wave and tidal currents, superimposed on stable, submerging (deepening) or shoaling conditions on shelf, with variation in sediment input. Modern shelves:
   relict sand blanket; sand shoals; ridge and swale sands; mud blanket.

   b) Inferred storm hydraulic regime associated with cape-associated shoal
   and shoal retreat massif (Figs. 14.3, 14.4).

   c) Sand bank (shoal) on mud-dominated shelf (Figs. 14.5-14.7).

   d) Tidal current dominated sand movement forming linear sand banks after
   Caston (Figs. 14.9-14.13).

   e) Sediment movement and sand distribution tidal inlet shoals, Sapelo
   Island area, Georgia; (Figs. 14.20-14.22; 12.6-12.8)

   f) Shallow wave activity and facies of sedimentary structures in high-
   energy nearshore (shore face) after Clifton, et al. (Figs. 14.14-14.17).

   g) Facies zonation of beach and nearshore environments, low wave energy
   coast, Sapelo Island, Georgia, after Howard and Reineck (Figs. 14.18-
   14.20).

   h. Wave reworking of abandoned delta front to give thin transgressive

(destructional) sheet sands. May be on shelf or overlapping older
delta plain (by submergence of marine water).

    i) Reworking of older coastal plain deposits on shelf because of sub-
mergence. Thin palimpsest sand - Holocene record on some modern
shelves.

    j) Characteristics of marine-shelf sand bodies (Table 8.5).

3. Tectonics and sedimentation:

    a) Types of shelves and tectonic control on origin.

    b) Local structural movement on shelf influencing water depth and producing
sand shoals.

    c) Localization of linear offshore bars on fault, anticlinal or diapiric
trends (brings water depth within effective wave base) (Fig. 14.7).

    d) Tectonic control on rates of deposition (Rd) compared with rates of
subsidence (Rs). Influence on transgressive and regressive movement
of shoreline and development of widespread shelf sands (Fig. 14.30,
14.31).

4. Importance of shallow marine sands in petroleum exploration.

    a) Most important petroleum-producing sandstones in many provinces.

    b) Close proximity of reservoir rock to adequate source rock favors
stratigraphically controlled accumulations.

    c) Shoreline sand trends have high predictability; offshore sand bars have
low predictability of trend, except those trends that are structurally
controlled.

    d) Thickness of single genetic unit containing reservoir rock commonly
20 to 30 feet thick (controlled by effective wave base). Multiple
units may develop in growth fault areas. Reservoir quality may be poor
to excellent.

5. Not important in coal exploration; of minor importance in uranium exploration.

6. Examples of ancient petroleum-producing sequences.

    a) Upper Cretaceous, Cardium Sandstone, Pembina Field, Alberta; 1.6 billion
bbls., largest field in Canada; Figs. 14.23-14.29.

    b) Upper Cretaceous, Frontier Sandstone, Salt Creek Field, Wyoming;
500,000,000 bbls., largest field in Rocky Mountain Region; Figs. 14.30
to 14.33.

    c) Lower Cretaceous, "J" Sandstone Fields, Nebraska; several 5 to 10
million bbl. fields; Figs. 14.34-14.42.

d) Lower Cretaceous, "J" Sandstone, Wattenberg Field, Colorado; 1.1
   trillion cu. ft. gas; largest gas field in Colorado; Figs. 14.45-14.49.

e) Upper Cretaceous, "Hygiene Sandstones" (Terry Sandstone), Spindle Field,
   Denver Basin Colorado; Fig. 14.50.

7. Examples of shallow water marine sandstone available for study during
   seminar: Outcrop - "Hygiene" Sandstones; Cores - Terry and Hygiene
   Sandstones, Spindle Field, Colorado (Upper Cretaceous); Codell (Frontier)
   Sandstone (Upper Cretaceous) Colorado; "J" Sandstone, Wattenberg Field,
   Colorado (Lower Cretaceous).

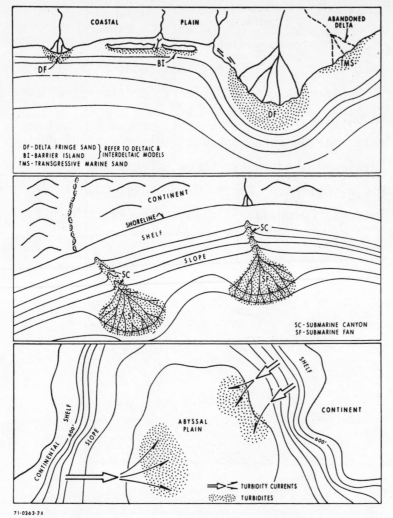

FIG. 14.1 Deposition of sand in marine environments.

After LeBlanc, 1972

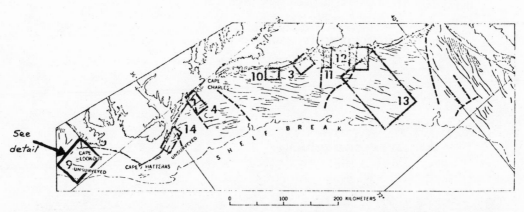

FIG. 14.2 Crest line of the more prominent ridges of the Middle Atlantic Bight, and the courses of the major shelf-transverse valleys. Boxes indicate locations of other figures. (Modified from Uchupi, 1968.)

After Swift, et al., 1973

144

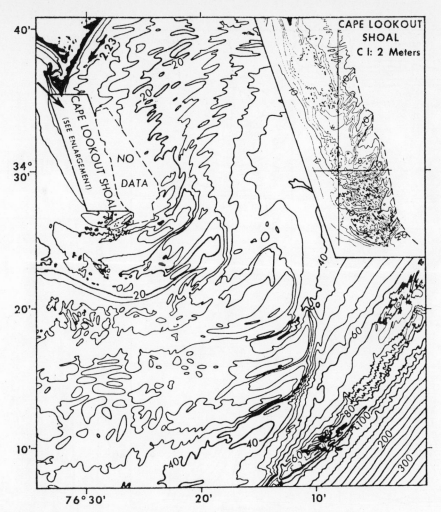

FIG. 14.3 Cape Lookout Shoal, a cape-associated shoal and shoal-retreat massif. Massif has been molded into arcuate transverse ridges, separated by swales which serve as storm spillways. Ridges have been flexed into an arcuate shape by wave refraction. They represent the third major mode of ridge formation. Littoral drift in cu. yd/yr × 10³ from Langfelder et al., (1968). Contours in meters.

INFERRED STORM HYDRAULIC REGIME

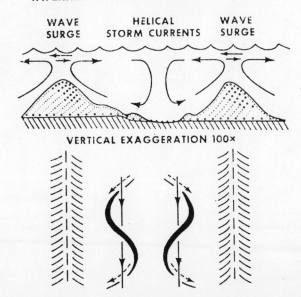

FIG. 14.4 Schematic diagram of secondary flow motions (helical flow structure) and storm wave surge believed to be associated with storm flow field.

After Swift, et al., 1973

145

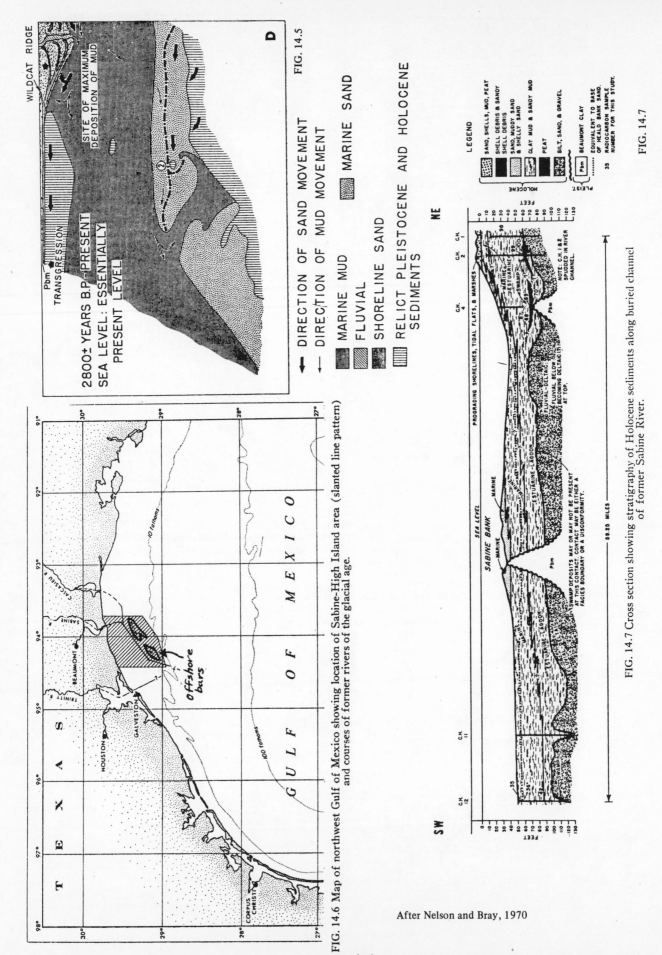

DIRECTION OF SAND MOVEMENT

DIRECTION OF MUD MOVEMENT

MARINE MUD

FLUVIAL

SHORELINE SAND

RELICT PLEISTOCENE AND HOLOCENE SEDIMENTS

MARINE SAND

2800± YEARS B.P. PRESENT
SEA LEVEL: ESSENTIALLY PRESENT LEVEL

SITE OF MAXIMUM DEPOSITION OF MUD

TRANSGRESSION

WILDCAT RIDGE

FIG. 14.5

FIG. 14.6 Map of northwest Gulf of Mexico showing location of Sabine-High Island area (slanted line pattern) and courses of former rivers of the glacial age.

LEGEND

SAND, SHELLS, MUD, PEAT

SHELL DEBRIS & SAND
SHELL DEBRIS

SAND, MUDDY SAND & SHELLY SAND

CLAY MUD & SANDY MUD

PEAT

SILT, SAND, & GRAVEL

HOLOCENE

Pbm BEAUMONT CLAY PLEIST.

.... EQUIVALENT TO BASE OF HEALD BANK SAND.

35 RADIOCARBON SAMPLE NUMBER FOR THIS STUDY.

FIG. 14.7

FIG. 14.7 Cross section showing stratigraphy of Holocene sediments along buried channel of former Sabine River.

After Nelson and Bray, 1970

146

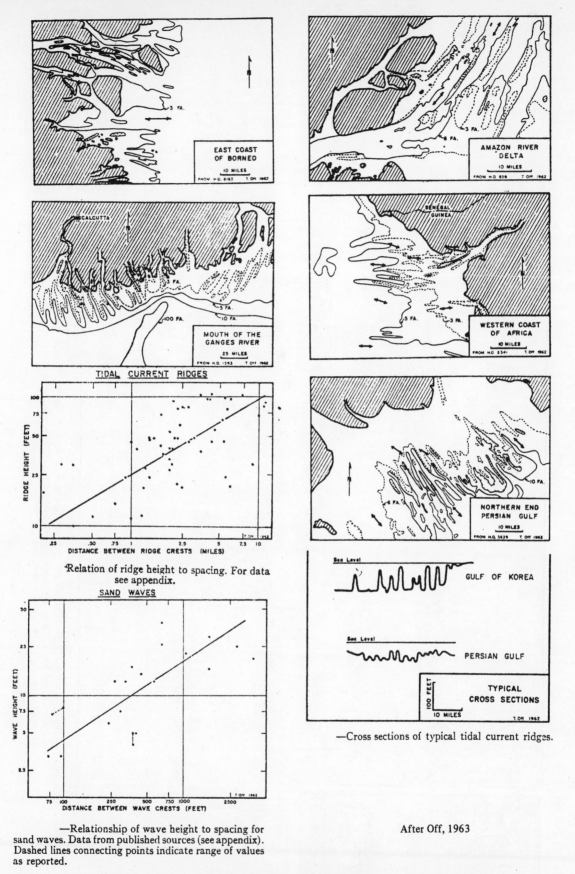

EAST COAST
OF BORNEO
10 MILES
FROM H.O. 6165   T OFF 1962

AMAZON RIVER
DELTA
10 MILES
FROM H.O. 839   T OFF 1962

MOUTH OF THE
GANGES RIVER
25 MILES
FROM H.O. 1593   T OFF 1962

WESTERN COAST
OF AFRICA
10 MILES
FROM H.O. 2341   T OFF 1962

TIDAL CURRENT RIDGES

Relation of ridge height to spacing. For data
see appendix.

SAND WAVES

NORTHERN END
PERSIAN GULF
10 MILES
FROM H.O. 3639   T OFF 1962

GULF OF KOREA

PERSIAN GULF

TYPICAL
CROSS SECTIONS
100 FEET
10 MILES   T OFF 1962

—Cross sections of typical tidal current ridges.

—Relationship of wave height to spacing for
sand waves. Data from published sources (see appendix).
Dashed lines connecting points indicate range of values
as reported.

After Off, 1963

FIG. 14.8—Diagrams and maps illustrating Tidal Current Ridges and Sand Waves.

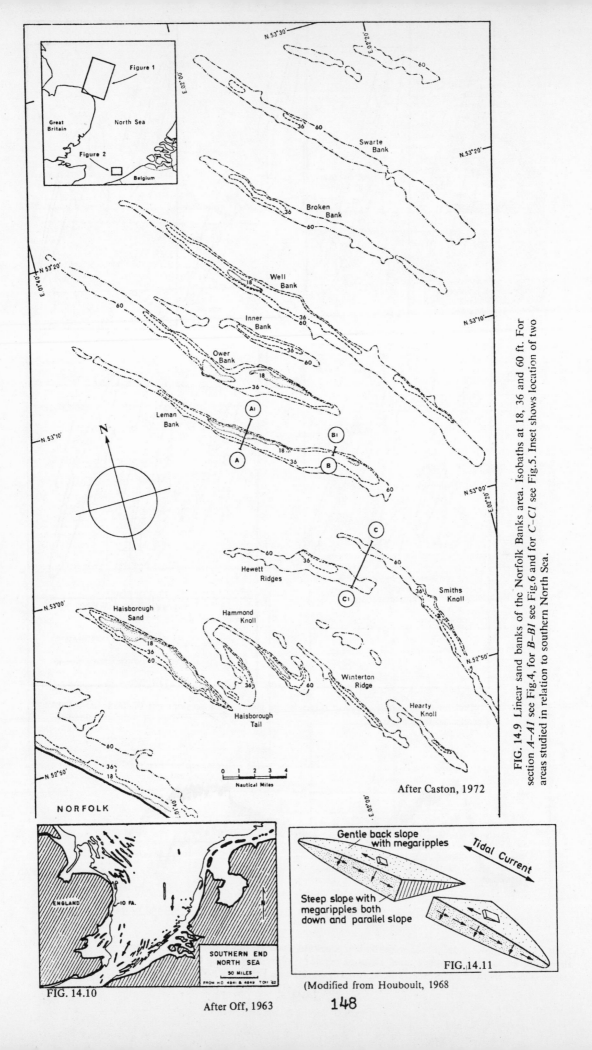

N.53°30'

E.02°20'

60

Swarte
Bank

N.53°20'

36 60

Broken
Bank

36

60

N.53°10'

Well
Bank

18

36
60

Inner
Bank

36
60

E.02°20'

Ower
Bank

36
60

18

36

N

Leman
Bank

A1

B1

18

A

36

B

60

N.53°20'

E.01°40'

60

N.53°10'

N.53°00'

E.02°20'

C

60

60

Hewett
Ridges

36

36

Smiths
Knoll

C1

N.53°00'

Haisborough
Sand

Hammond
Knoll

N.52°50'

18

36

60

36

Winterton
Ridge

60

Hearty
Knoll

36

Haisborough
Tail

60

E.02°00'

60

0 1 2 3 4
Nautical Miles

36

N.52°50'

18

E.01°40'

NORFOLK

After Caston, 1972

FIG. 14.9 Linear sand banks of the Norfolk Banks area. Isobaths at 18, 36 and 60 ft. For section *A–A1* see Fig.4, for *B–B1* see Fig.6 and for *C–C1* see Fig.5. Inset shows location of two areas studied in relation to southern North Sea.

ENGLAND

10 FA.

SOUTHERN END
NORTH SEA
50 MILES
FROM H.O 4941 & 4849 TOM '62

FIG. 14.10

After Off, 1963

Gentle back slope
with megaripples

Tidal Current

Steep slope with
megaripples both
down and parallel slope

FIG.14.11

(Modified from Houboult, 1968

148

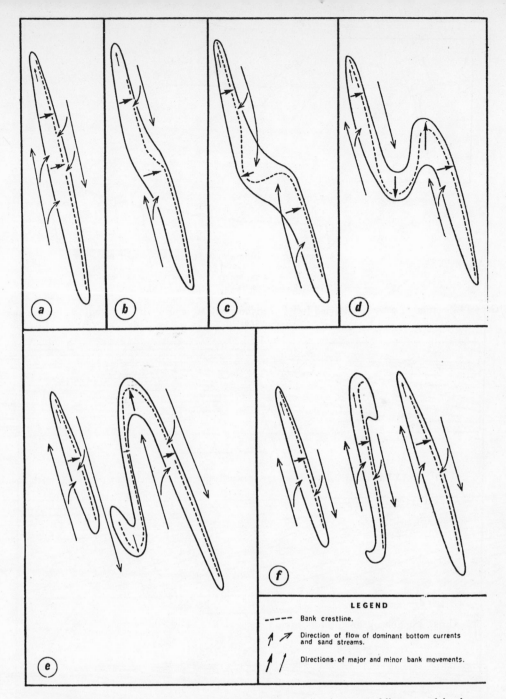

FIG. 14.12 Diagram showing stages in the growth and development of linear sand banks. For discussion, see text.

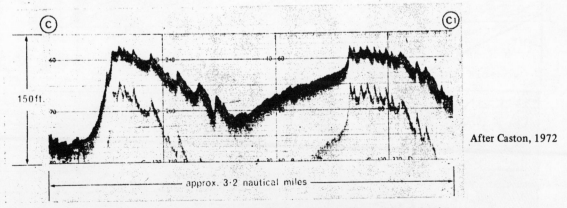

After Caston, 1972

FIG. 14.13 Echo-sounder profile across Smiths Knoll (left) and Hewett Ridges (right) showing abundance of large, asymmetric, sand waves on gentle (southwesterly facing) bank slopes. The steeper sides of the sand waves face up-slope, towards the crestline. For location of C–C1, see Fig.

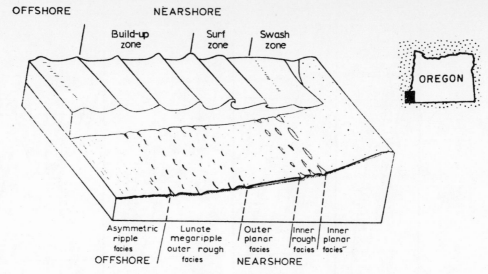

OFFSHORE NEARSHORE

Build-up zone   Surf zone   Swash zone

OREGON

Asymmetric ripple facies | Lunate megaripple outer rough facies | Outer planar facies | Inner rough facies | Inner planar facies

OFFSHORE   NEARSHORE

FIG. 14.14 Zonation of wave activity and facies of sedimentary structures within and adjacent to the high-energy nearshore.

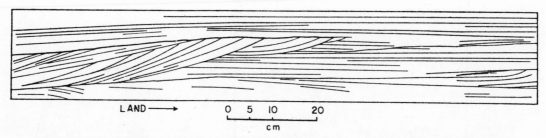

LAND →   0 5 10   20
cm

FIG. 14.15 Internal structures from the seaweed edge of the inner planar facies (swash zone).

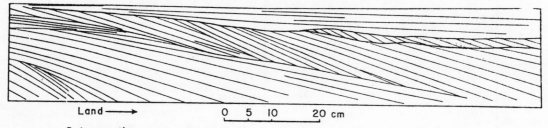

Land →   0 5 10   20 cm

a. Outer portion outer planar facies

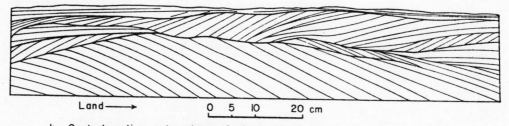

Land →   0 5 10   20 cm

b. Central portion outer planar facies

FIG. 14.16 Internal structures from the outer planar facies.

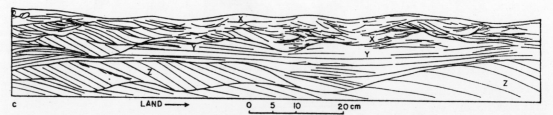

c   LAND →   0 5 10   20 cm

FIG. 14.17 Internal structure of sand just seaward from the offshore-nearshore boundary on an average day.

Clifton, et al., 1971

150

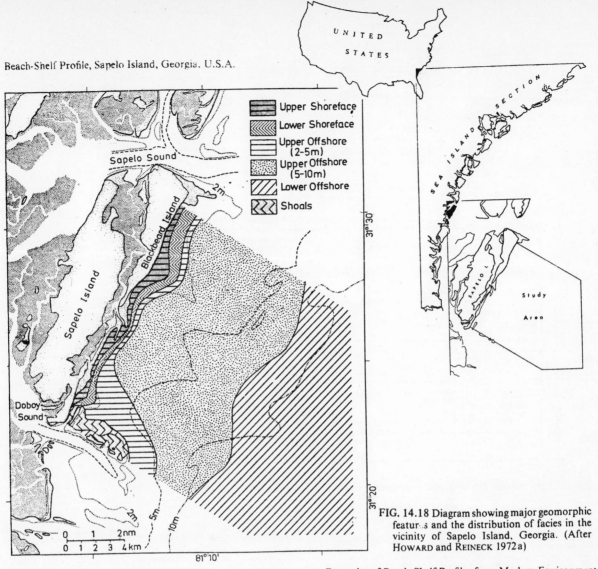

FIG. 14.18 Diagram showing major geomorphic features and the distribution of facies in the vicinity of Sapelo Island, Georgia. (After HOWARD and REINECK 1972a)

Examples of Beach-Shelf Profiles from Modern Environments

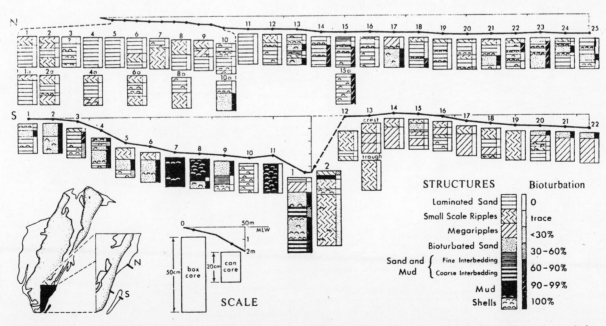

FIG. 14.19 Geographic representation of can cores. Various sedimentary structures found in each can core profile are shown by symbols for each station. The degree of bioturbation is shown on the right of the column of the can-core profile. (After HOWARD and REINECK, 1972a)

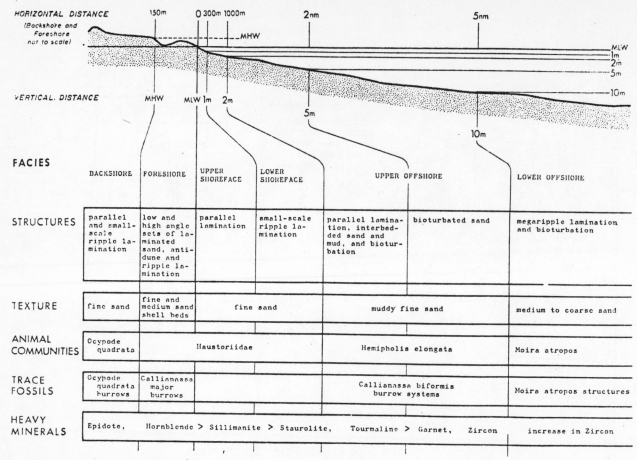

FIG. 14.20 Facies zonation of the beach and near shore environments, Sapelo Island, Georgia. (After HOWARD and REINECK, 1972a)

	BACKSHORE	FORESHORE	UPPER SHOREFACE	LOWER SHOREFACE	UPPER OFFSHORE		LOWER OFFSHORE
STRUCTURES	parallel and small-scale ripple lamination	low and high angle sets of laminated sand, antidune and ripple lamination	parallel lamination	small-scale ripple lamination	parallel lamination, interbedded sand and mud, and bioturbation	bioturbated sand	megaripple lamination and bioturbation
TEXTURE	fine sand	fine and medium sand shell beds	fine sand		muddy fine sand		medium to coarse sand
ANIMAL COMMUNITIES	Ocypode quadrata	Haustoriidae			Hemipholis elongata		Moira atropos
TRACE FOSSILS	Ocypode quadrata burrows	Callianassa major burrows			Callianassa biformis burrow systems		Moira atropos structures
HEAVY MINERALS	Epidote,	Hornblende > Sillimanite > Staurolite,			Tourmaline > Garnet, Zircon		increase in Zircon

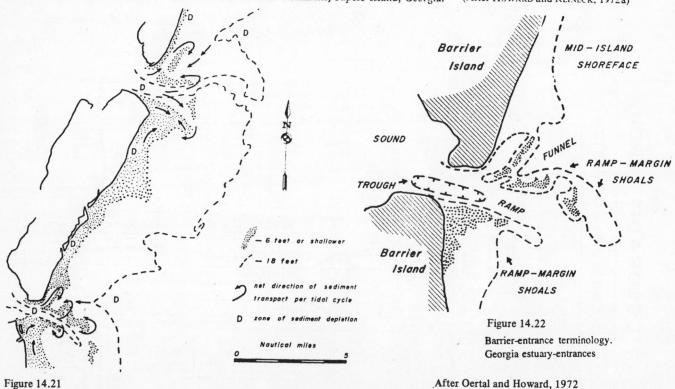

Figure 14.21

Pattern of sediment movement and depletion adjacent estuary-entrance shoals. At estuary entrances, sediment becomes trapped in a closed system and shoal progradation takes place at the expense of the adjacent beach, shoreface, and tidal channels.

Figure 14.22

Barrier-entrance terminology.
Georgia estuary-entrances

After Oertal and Howard, 1972

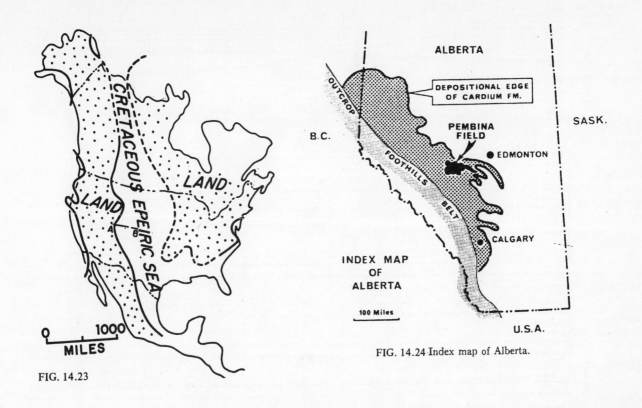

FIG. 14.23

FIG. 14.24 Index map of Alberta.

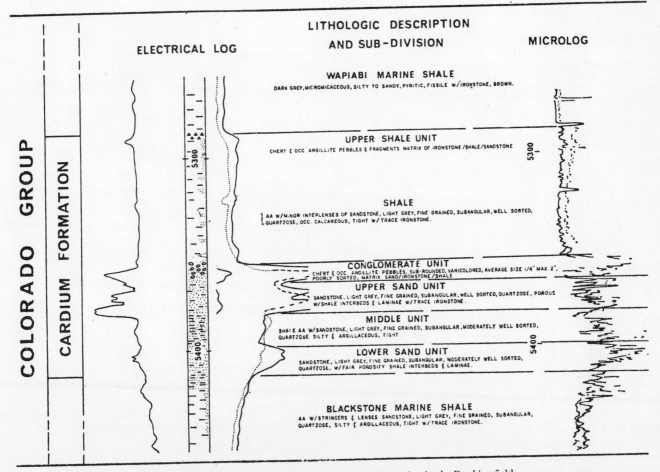

FIG. 14.25 Detail log of typical Cardium Formation in the Pembina field.

After Mills, 1968

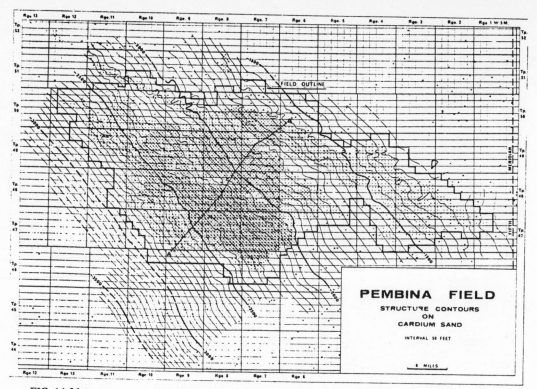

FIG. 14.26 Structure map of the Pembina field, contoured on the Cardium sand. Interval is 50 ft.

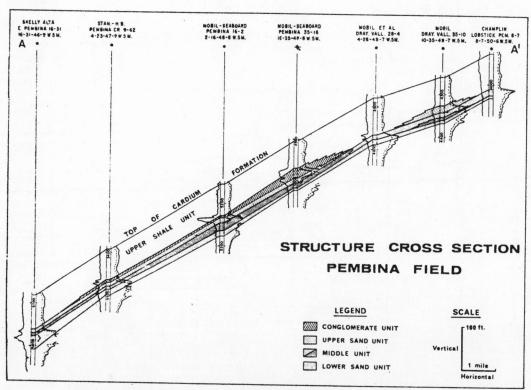

FIG. 14.27 Structure cross section of Pembina field. Trace is A-A' on Figs. . and . .

After Mills, 1968

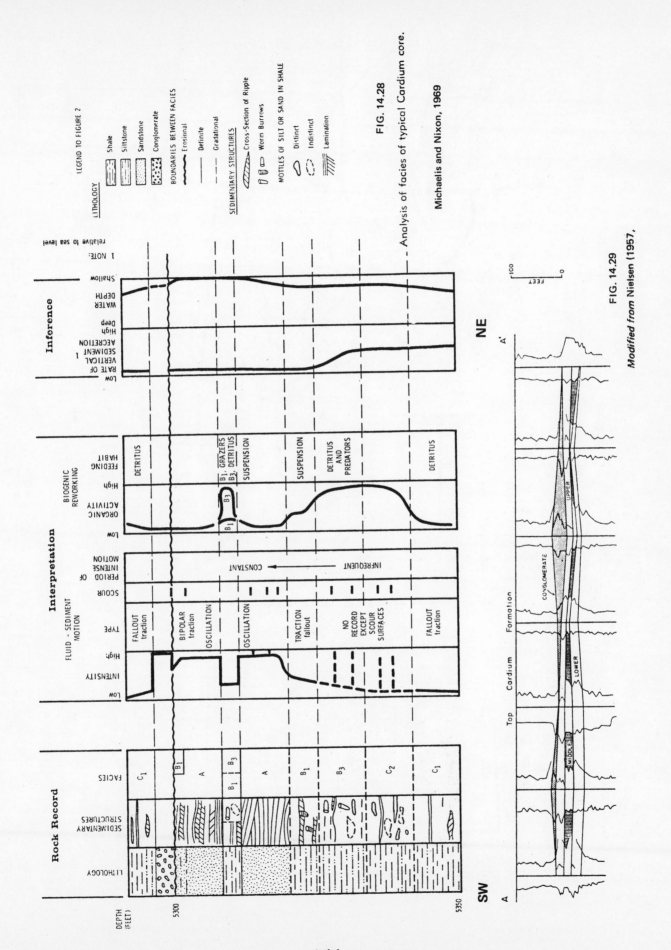

FIG. 14.28

Analysis of facies of typical Cardium core.

Michaelis and Nixon, 1969

FIG. 14.29

Modified from Nielsen (1957,

155

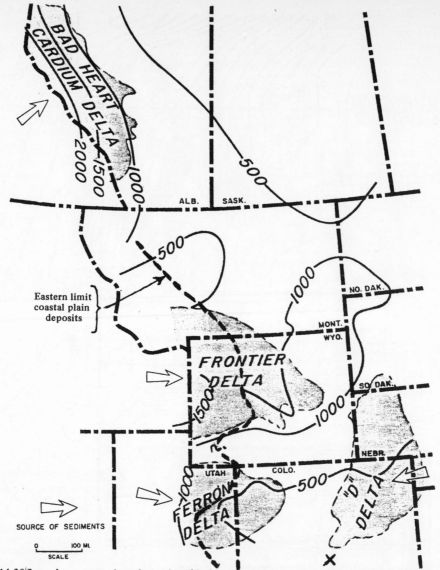

FIG. 14.30 Isopachous map of total stratigraphic interval between top of Mowry Shale and base of Niobrara Formation (or time equivalent where possible). Formation names in areas of major sandstone concentration are indicated. Contours in feet.

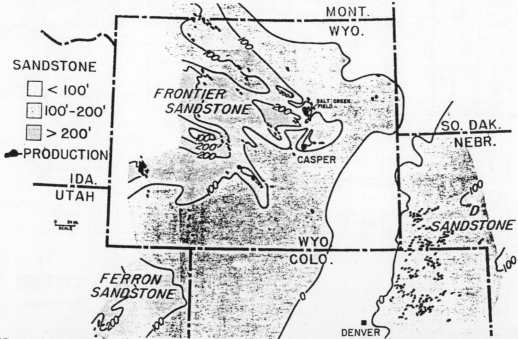

FIG. 14.31 Isopachous map of total sandstone within Frontier and correlative formations. Codell Sandstone Member of Benton Shale, on southeast, is omitted from computations. Contours in feet.

Modified after Barlow & Haun, 1966

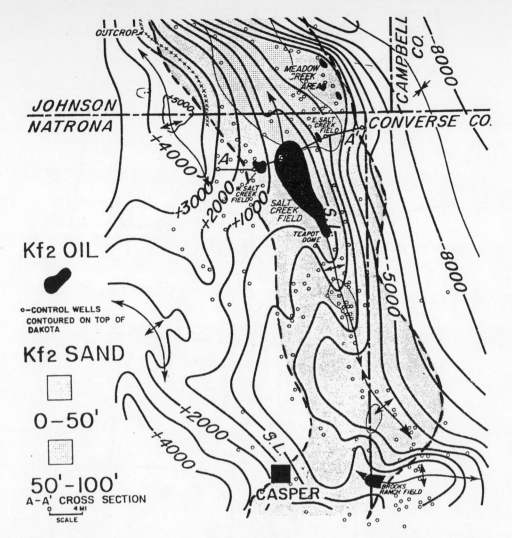

Kf2 OIL

o–CONTROL WELLS
CONTOURED ON TOP OF
DAKOTA

Kf2 SAND

☐ 0–50'

☐ 50'–100'

A–A' CROSS SECTION

SCALE 0 4 MI

FIG. 14.32 Structure of southwest Powder River basin (structural datum to top of Dakota), distribution of second Frontier sandstone (Kf₂), and oil fields in second Frontier sandstone. Contours in feet above and below sea-level.

WEST   A – A'   EAST

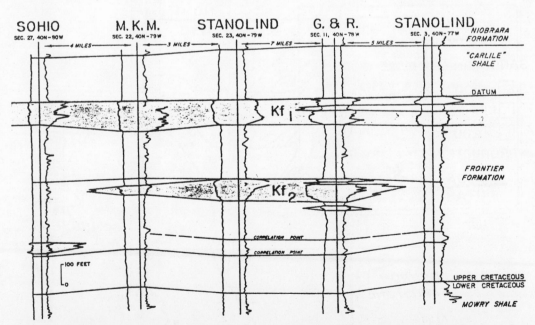

FIG. 14.33 West-east electric-log cross section A-A' of Frontier Formation showing correlation of first Frontier (Kf₁) and second Frontier (Kf₂) sandstones, and associated shale and siltstone. See Figure 6 for location of section.

After Barlow and Haun, 1966

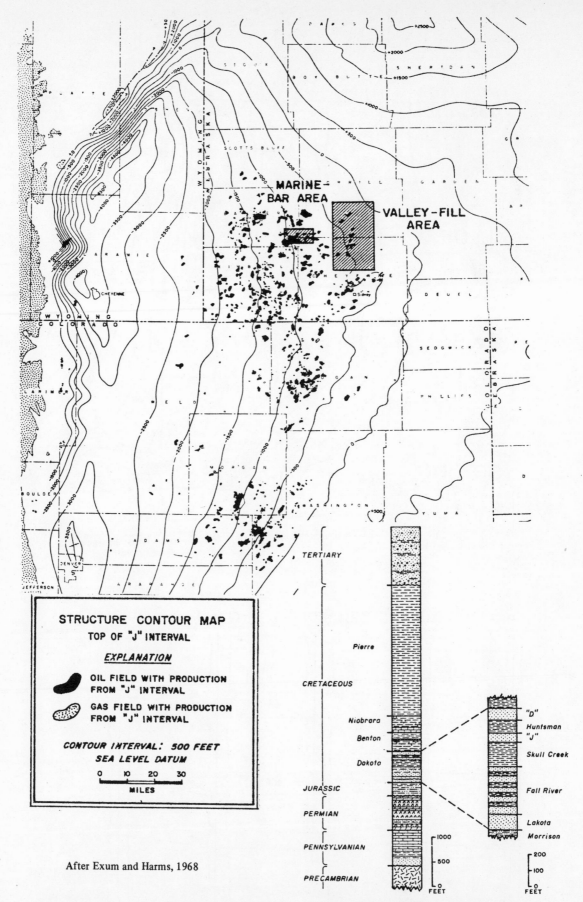

STRUCTURE CONTOUR MAP

TOP OF "J" INTERVAL

EXPLANATION

OIL FIELD WITH PRODUCTION
FROM "J" INTERVAL

GAS FIELD WITH PRODUCTION
FROM "J" INTERVAL

CONTOUR INTERVAL: 500 FEET
SEA LEVEL DATUM

0   10   20   30
MILES

After Exum and Harms, 1968

FIG. 14.35 Generalized stratigraphic column,
western Nebraska.

FIG. 14.34 Structural contour map of Denver basin. Datum is top of Dakota (Cretaceous) "J" interval. Depth datum is sea level. Cross-hatched blocks show marine-bar and valley-fill study areas. CI = 500 ft.

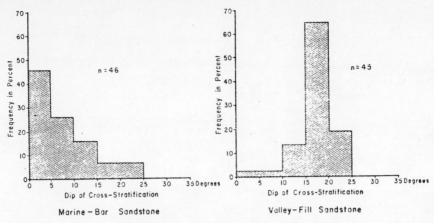

FIG. 14.36 Histograms showing dip of large-scale cross-stratification for marine-bar and valley-fill rocks. Although range of dips is same, more than 80 percent of dips in marine bar are less than 15° and more than 80 percent of dips in valley fill are greater than 15°.

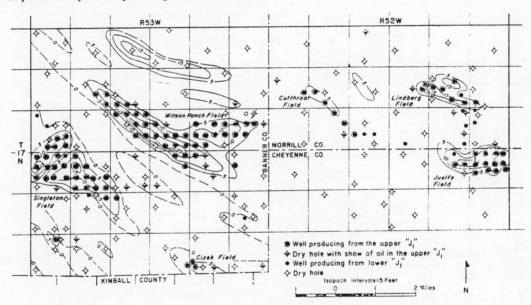

FIG. 14.37 Isopach map of net sandstone in upper "J₁," marine-bar area, Nebraska. CI = 5 ft.

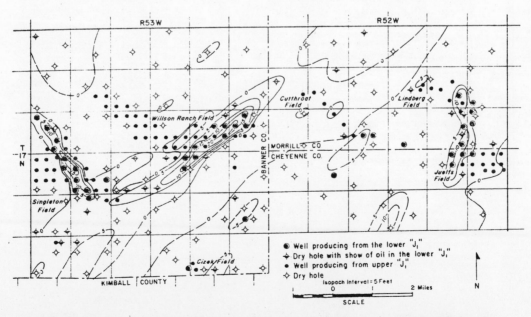

FIG. 14.38 Isopach map of net sandstone in lower "J₁," marine-bar area, Nebraska. CI = 5 ft.

After Exum and Harms, 1968

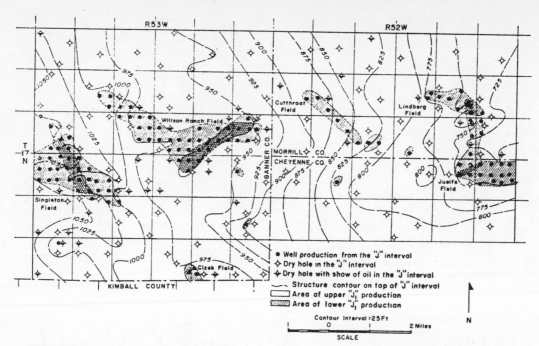

FIG. 14.39 Subsea structure contours, datum top of "J" unit, marine-bar area, Nebraska. Depth datum is sea level. Upper and lower "J₁" productive areas are shown by hatched patterns. Prdouction clearly is not related to structural closure. CI = 25 ft.

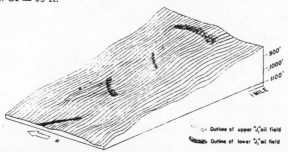

FIG. 14.40 Isometric block diagram of marine-bar study area with productive limits outlined for upper and lower "J₁" reservoirs. Structural relief is represented by lines formed by intersection of top of "J" unit with regularly spaced east-west vertical planes. Oil accumulations are independent of structural closure.

ROCK PROPERTIES

	MARINE BAR	VALLEY FILL
MINERALOGY	GLAUCONITE PRESENT	GLAUCONITE ABSENT
TEXTURES	CLAY CONTENT DECREASES UPWARD PEBBLES RARE	CLAY CONTENT INCREASES UPWARD PEBBLES COMMON
STRUCTURES	LOW-ANGLE CROSS STRATA SYMMETRIC RIPPLES BURROWED	HIGH-ANGLE CROSS STRATA ASYMMETRIC RIPPLES DEFORMED
PALEONTOLOGY	MARINE MICROFOSSILS, POLLEN, SPORES	SPORES, POLLEN

FIG. 14.41 Comparison of rock properties of marine bars and valley fill.

RESERVOIR GEOMETRY

	MARINE BAR	VALLEY FILL
WIDTH	~0.5-1.5 MILES	~0.3-0.4 MILES
LENGTH	< 6 MILES	> 20 MILES
THICKNESS	25 FEET MAXIMUM	80 FEET MAXIMUM
FORM	SCATTERED ELLIPTICAL LENSES	SINGLE LONG PRISM
LATERAL CHANGE	DEPOSITIONAL, GRADATIONAL	EROSIONAL, ABRUPT
BASAL CONTACT	TRANSITIONAL OR SHARP	EROSIONAL

FIG. 14.42 Comparison of reservoir geometry of marine bars and valley fill.

EXPLORATION GUIDELINES

	MARINE BAR	VALLEY FILL
ENTRAPMENT	STRATIGRAPHIC	STRUCTURE REQUIRED
BARRIER LITHOLOGY	COMMONLY ADEQUATE, OIL COLUMNS >100 FT	LESS ADEQUATE, OIL COLUMNS <50 FT
PROXIMITY	GRADIENTS IN CLAY CONTENT	NO INDICATION
TARGET WIDTH	~0.5-1.5 MILES	~1000-2000 FEET
TREND PROJECTION	UNCERTAIN	GOOD

FIG. 14.43 Comparison of exploration guidelines for marine bars and valley fill.

PRODUCTION CHARACTERISTICS

	MARINE BAR	VALLEY FILL
MAXIMUM EXPECTED IN-PLACE RESERVES	40 MILLION BBL	10 MILLION BBL
ENERGY	SOLUTION GAS	WATER DRIVE
PRIMARY RECOVERY	LOW	HIGH
RESERVOIR HOMOGENEITY	HIGH	LOW

FIG. 14.44 Comparison of production characteristics of marine bars and valley fill.

160

After Exum and Harms, 1968

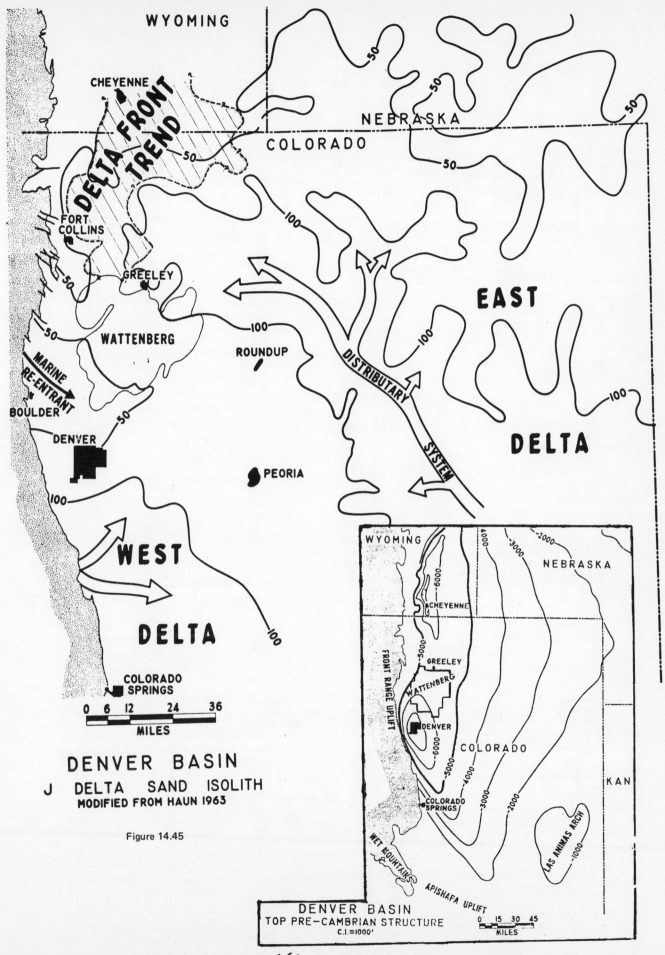

WYOMING

CHEYENNE

DELTA FRONT TREND

NEBRASKA

COLORADO

FORT COLLINS

50

GREELEY

EAST

WATTENBERG

100

ROUNDUP

DISTRIBUTARY

MARINE RE-ENTRANT

BOULDER

50

DENVER

PEORIA

100

DELTA

SYSTEM

100

WEST

DELTA

100

COLORADO SPRINGS

0 6 12   24   36
MILES

DENVER BASIN
J DELTA SAND ISOLITH
MODIFIED FROM HAUN 1963

Figure 14.45

WYOMING

4000

-2000

NEBRASKA

3000

CHEYENNE

5000

GREELEY

WATTENBERG

FRONT RANGE UPLIFT

6000

6000

DENVER

COLORADO

5000

KAN

4000

COLORADO SPRINGS

3000

2000

WET MOUNTAINS

LAS ANIMAS ARCH

1000

APISHAFA UPLIFT

DENVER BASIN
TOP PRE-CAMBRIAN STRUCTURE
C.I.=1000'

0 15 30 45
MILES

161   After Matuszczak, 1973

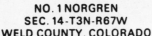

NO. 1 NORGREN
SEC. 14-T3N-R67W
WELD COUNTY, COLORADO

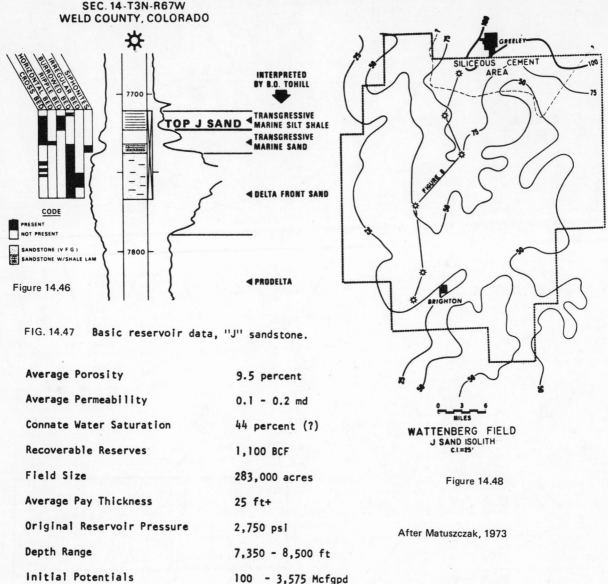

Figure 14.46

FIG. 14.47 Basic reservoir data, "J" sandstone.

Average Porosity	9.5 percent
Average Permeability	0.1 - 0.2 md
Connate Water Saturation	44 percent (?)
Recoverable Reserves	1,100 BCF
Field Size	283,000 acres
Average Pay Thickness	25 ft+
Original Reservoir Pressure	2,750 psi
Depth Range	7,350 - 8,500 ft
Initial Potentials	100 - 3,575 Mcfgpd

WATTENBERG FIELD
J SAND ISOLITH
C.I.=25'

Figure 14.48

After Matuszczak, 1973

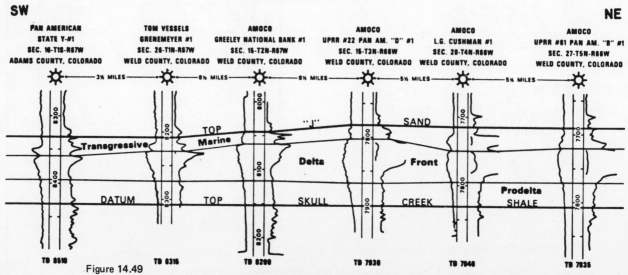

Figure 14.49

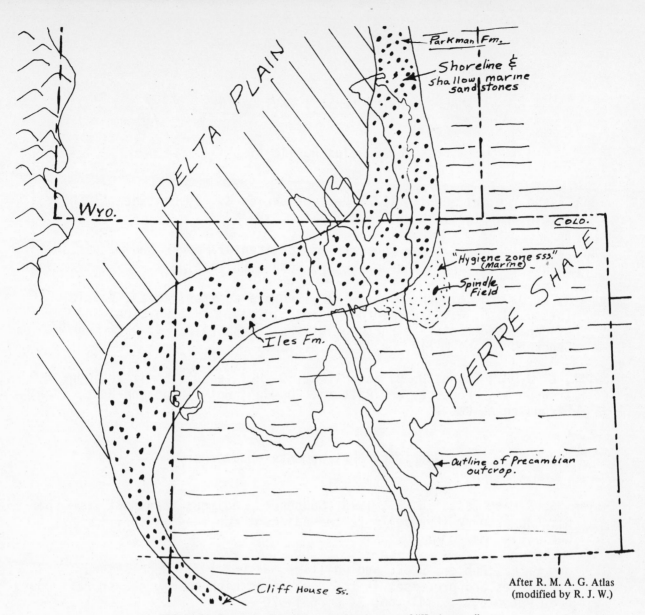

FIG. 14.50 Campanian lithofacies map showing area of "Hygiene sss."

After R. M. A. G. Atlas
(modified by R. J. W.)

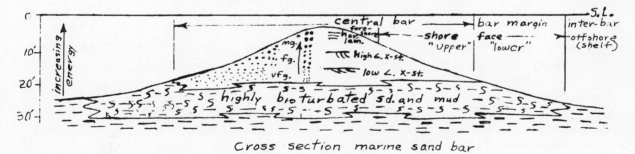

Cross section marine sand bar

Longitudinal section showing accretion down axis of bar.

FIG. 14.51 Diagram showing similarity of facies and terminology of marine bar to shoreface.

163

SHALLOW MARINE (SHELF) ENVIRONMENTS

Books or Special Publications

Amer. Assoc. Petrol. Geol., 1972, Reprint Series No. 3, Continental Shelves Origin and Significance, Tulsa, Okla., 194 p.

Amer. Geological Inst., New Concepts of Continental Margin Sedimentation, Wash., D. C., Short Course Lecture Notes, Philadelphia, Nov. 7-9, 1969.

*Howard, J. D. and Reineck, H. E., 1972, Georgia coastal region, Sapelo Island, U. S. A.: sedimentology and biology. IV, Physical and biogenic sedimentary structures of the nearshore shelf: Senckenbergiana Marit., v. 4, p. 81-123.

Swift, D. J. P., Duane, D. B. and Pilkey, O. H., (eds.), Shelf sediment transport: Processes and Pattern: Dowden, Hutchinson and Ross, Inc., Stroudsburg, Pa.

Shelf (Neritic) Environments--Quaternary

Allen, G. P. and Castaing, P., 1973, Suspended sediment transport from the Gironde estuary (France) onto the adjacent continental shelf: Mar. Geol., 14, M47-M53.

*Clifton, H. E., Hunter, R. E. and Phillips, R. L., 1971, Depositional structures and processes in the non-barred high-energy nearshore: Jour. Sed. Petrology, v. 41, no. 3, p. 651-670

*Caston, V. N. D., 1972, Linear sand banks in the southern North Sea: Sedimentology, v. 13, p. 63-78.

Caston, V. N. D., and Stride, A. H., 1970, Tidal sand movement between some linear sand banks in the North Sea off northeast Norfolk: Mar. Geol., v. 9, M38-M42.

Curray, J. R., 1965, Late Quaternary history, continental shelves of the United States: in Quaternary of the United States: Wright, H. E. and Frey, D. G (eds). Princeton Univ. Press, p. 723-735.

Dingle, R. V., 1965, Sand waves in the North Sea mapped by continuous reflection profiling: Mar. Geol., v. 3, no. 6, p. 391-400.

Emory, K. O., 1952, Continental shelf sediments of Southern California: Geol. Soc. Amer. Bull., v. 63, p. 1106-1108.

_____, 1968, Relict sediments on continental shelves of world: Amer. Assoc. Petrol. Geol. Bull., v. 52, p. 445-464. (also in AAPG Reprint Series No. 3).

Emory, K. O., 1969, The continental shelves: Scientific Amer., v. 221, no. 3, p. 106-122.

_____, 1971, Bottom sediment map of the Malacca Strait: Tech. Bull., E.C.A.F.E., v. 4, p. 149-152.

Ewing, J. A., 1973, Wave induced bottom currents on the outer shelf: Mar. Geol., v. 14, p. M31-M35.

Gorsline, D. S., 1963, Bottom sediments of the Atlantic shelf and slope off southern United States: Jour. Geol., v. 71, p. 442-447.

Hallam, A., (ed.), 1967, Depth indicators in marine sedimentary environments: Mr. Geol., v. 5 (special issue), p. 329-567.

Houboult, J. J. H. C., 1968, Recent sediments in the southern bight of the North Sea: Geol. Mijnbauw, v. 47, p. 245-273.

Jones, N. S., Kain, J. M. and Stride, A. H., 1965, The movement of sand waves on Warts Bank, Isle of Man: Mar. Geol., v. 3, no. 5, p. 329-336.

Keller, G. K. and Richards, A. F., 1967, Sediment of the Malacca Strait; southeast area: Jour. Sed. Petrology, v. 37, 1, pp. 102-127.

Kenyon, N. H., 1970, Sand ribbons of European tidal seas: Mar. Geol., v. 9, p. 25-39.

Kenyon, N. H. and Stride, A. H., 1970, The tide-swept continental shelf sediments between the Shetland Islands and France: Sedimentology, v. 14, p. 159-173.

Nelson, H. F. and Bray, E. E., 1970, Stratigraphy and history of the Holocene sediments in the Sabine-High Island area, Gulf of Mexico: in Morgan, J. P. (ed.), Deltaic Sedimentation, Modern and Ancient: Soc. Econ. Paleo and Min. Sp. Pub. 15, p. 48-77.

Off, T., 1963, Rythmic linear sand bodies caused by tidal currents: Amer. Assoc. Petrol. Geol. Bull., v. 47, p. 332-341.

Oertal, G. F., II, and Howard, J. D., 1972, Water circulation and sedimentation at estuary entrances on the Georgia Coast: in Swift, et al. (eds.), Shelf Sediment Transport: process and pattern, Dowden, Hutchinson and Ross, Inc. Stroudsburg, Pa.

Reineck, H. E., 1963, Sedimentary structures (stratification) in the area of the southern North Sea: Senckenberg Research Inst. for Marine Geology and Marine Biology, Publ. no. 217, 138 p. (published in German).

Smith, J. D., 1969, Geomorphology of a sand ridge: Jour. Geology, v. 77, p. 39-55.

Stanley, D. J., Curray, J. R., Middleton, F. V. and Swift, D. J. P., 1969, The new concepts of continental margin sedimentation: Amer. Geol. Inst., Short Course Lecture Notes, Wash., D. C.

Stride, A. H., 1963, Current-swept sea floors near the southern half of Great Britain: Quart. Jour. Geol. Soc. London: v. 119, p. 175-199.

Stride, A. H. and Chesterman, W. D., 1973, Sedimentation by non-tidal currents around northern Denmark: Mar. Geol., v. 15, M53-M58.

*Swift, D. J. P., Duane, D. B. and McKinney, T. F., 1973, Ridge and swale topography of the middle Atlantic Bight, North America: secular response to the Holocene hydraulic regime: Mar. Geol. v. 15, p. 227-247.

Swift, D. J. P., Stanley, D. J., and Curray, J. R., 1971, Relict sediments on continental shelves: a reconsideration: Jour. Geol., v. 79, p. 322-346.

Terwindt, J. H. J., 1971, Sand waves in the southern bight of the North Sea: Mar. Geol., v. 10, no. 1, p. 51-69.

Uchupi, E., 1968, The Atlantic continental shelf and slope of the United States: physiography: U. S. Geol. Survey Prof. Paper 529--C, p. 1-20.

Van Stratten, L. M. J. U., 1959, Minor structures of some recent littoral and neritic sediments: Geol. en Mijnbauw, v. 21, p. 197-216.

Shallow Marine (Neritic) Deposits - Ancient

*Barlow, J. A., Jr. and Haun, J. D., 1966, Regional stratigraphy of Frontier Formation and relation to Salt Creek Field, Wyoming: Amer. Assoc. Petrol. Geol. Bull., v. 50, no. 10, 2185-2196.

Berven, R. J., 1966, Cardium sandstone bodies, Crossfield-Garrington: Bull. Canadian Petrol. Geol., v. 14, no. 2, p. 208-240.

Cobban, W. A. and Reside, J. B., Jr., 1952, Frontier Formation, Wyoming and adjacent areas: Amer. Assoc. Petrol. Geol. Bull., v. 36, no. 10, p. 1913-1961.

Evans, W. E., 1970, Imbricate linear sandstone bodies of Viking Formation in Dodsland - Hoosier area of Southwestern Saskatchewan, Canada: Amer. Assoc. Petrol. Geol. Bull., v. 54, no. 3, p. 469-486.

*Exum, F. A. and Harms, J. C., 1968, Comparison of marine-bar with valley-fill stratigraphic traps, Western Nebraska: Amer. Assoc. Petrol. Geol. Bull., v. 52, no. 10, p. 1851-1868.

*Howard, J. D., 1972, Trace fossils as criteria for recognizing shorlines in stratigraphic record: Soc. Econ. Paleo. and Min. Sp. Pub. 16, p. 215-225.

*Matuszczak, R. A., 1973, Wattenberg field, Denver Basin, Colorado: The Mountain Geologist, v. 10, no. 3, p. 99-105.

Michaelis, E. R., 1957, Cardium sedimentation in the Pembina River area: Alberta Soc. Petrol. Geol., Jour., v. 5, p. 73-77.

*Michaelis, E. R. and Nixon, G., 1969, Interpretation of depositional pro - cesses from sedimentary structures in the Cardium sand: Canad. Petrol. Geol. Bull., v. 17, no. 4, p. 410-443.

Mills, B. A., 1968, Solution-gas reserves in Pembina Cardium oil field, Alberta Canada: Amer. Assoc. Petrol. Geol. Memoir 9, p. 698-704.

Nielsen, A. R., 1957, Cardium stratigraphy of the Pembina Field: Alberta Soc. Petrol. Geol. Jour., v. 5, no. 4, p. 64-72.

Patterson, A. M. and Arneson, A. A., 1957, Geology of Pembina Field, Alberta: Amer. Assoc. Petrol. Geol. Bull., v. 41, p. 937-949.

-- Notes --